Challenge What you Think

Believe What is Possible

Max Glover

First published in Great Britain in 2021 by Amazon

This edition published in 2022

2

Copyright © Max Glover 2021

ISBN 9798841267966

Independently published

This book is dedicated to:

- The staff at the Royal Brompton & Harefield Hospital who are doing an incredible job helping patients in desperate need of heart and lung transplants;

- Serving members and Veterans of the Armed Forces;

- To all those who have ever been told that they cannot achieve their goals.

"Impossible is temporary. Impossible is nothing."

-Muhammad Ali

Contents

Special Thanks To

My Mum

Alan King

Chris Mcjennett

Chris Probert

Jason King

Jules

Luke "The Coolest" Glover

Mark Camilleri

Mark Cole

Matthew Jones

Nez

Paul Webber

Samantha Rogers

Stephen Foster

Terry Rosoman

Rokman

Photo credits: Rokman

Pushed to
the Limit

Pushed to The Limit

My calves were scorched by painful lactic acid; my muscles leeched the red blood cells faster than my heart could supply. Constant beads of sweat trickled down my forehead, providing no relief to my overheating body. The sweat flowed down my cheeks and met on my chin, gathering their masses before dripping down to the floor to join the large pool of perspiration beneath me.

As I struggled to keep my breathing under control, I could not comprehend the unbelievable heat. There was no airflow. Air conditioning was not a thing in these days. I couldn't breathe. If there was a hell, this was it. But there was no escape.

Slightly in front of me and to the right was Johnny. I could see him in my peripheral vision. While not really a friend of mine he was more someone I knew, a boisterous lad and a well-known maverick. He was a few years older than me, fitter, stronger, more athletic. His blonde hair and dashing good looks quickly made way for a grimace as his complexion rapidly began to resemble that of a strawberry. He was in an even worse state than I was, his head hanging loosely down as he struggled to keep his composure. His movements becoming more erratic, sloppy, limp.

It soon dawned on me, that watching someone else absolutely hanging out, while I myself was in the hurt locker was quite a comforting experience. In a non-sadistic way, it actually made me feel a little better, I grew stronger and it gave me the drive to keep my head up and keep going. I bit the bullet and kept up the pace. Every fibre in my body began to scream. Was this nightmare ever going to end?

And there it came like a wailing banshee. Finally. A loud defeated groan erupted from behind me, piercing the dull sounds of heavy breathing that echoed around the hall. Someone had given up. This created a domino effect as seconds later behind me again another sound of failure, this time more like a whimper.

I glanced over at Johnny to see how he was getting on. His upper back was rounded, shoulders hunched forwards, panting heavily. My eyes locked onto his quivering legs just in time to watch him grind to a halt. He hunched forward, hands on his thighs as he began to wretch.

He turned to face me as the tears streamed down his face like Niagara Falls and I could see he had been well and truly broken. For a brief moment that felt like eternity we locked eyes, and I could see the pain and felt his defeat deep within my soul.

Johnny ran to the back of the hall calling for his mother. I returned my gaze to the front and cracked on. All around me boys were dropping like flies. I held my head up. Looking directly at the instructor.

Stood at the front was a young girl, possibly a teenager who had been well and truly pushed out of her depth. She was not a real instructor; in fact, she was a senior student. This was a Taekwondo lesson and the actual instructor was stuck in a traffic jam.

The young lady had been asked to fill in and take the warm up for the remaining 15 students. She started us off with jumping jacks, and 45 minutes later, with no stopping, no rest or water breaks we were still at it. I was 9 years old, and this was my first introduction to the true grit of pushing my limits.

Belief

Belief

Being bold enough to believe we can do something is the first step to achieving our goals. No matter how far-fetched they may initially appear.

The human body is stronger that we realise and can endure more than we give it credit for.

There is a saying and depending on the source is goes something like this:

Dream, Believe, Achieve

Or

Imagine, Believe, Achieve

Both these sayings however clichéd may be the same and very true. Without imagination or vision, we cannot think of what we wish to do. Without belief in ourselves we simply cannot do it.

This whole book is about my story of tough, physical challenges that all began with an idea. I want you to join me on the journey as I take you from the initial spark in my mind all the way to the end of my challenge.

I hope you enjoy reading about my journey as much I enjoyed pursuing it.

Who is Max Glover?

A little introduction about me! I imagine those of you who are reading this will have either met me or watched some of my challenge videos or bought some of my exercise programmes.

I'd like to give a bit background just so you know the sort of guy you have just bought a book off (hopefully this won't lead to an influx of returns!)

At the time of writing this book I am 34 years old and working as a full time Personal Trainer and a part time challenge enthusiast! I was tempted to add "aspiring Author" to the list, but I will leave you to be the judge of that!

I grew up in the seaside town of Penarth, which is in South Wales, UK right next to Cardiff. I was never particularly interested in sport or fitness as a teenager, and I was certainly not gifted with many skills. Quite often, during Physical Education class I was the last to be picked in football because nobody wanted me on their team. I don't blame them, because quite frankly, I was crap.

In fact, when eventually I was picked for the side – despite my protests I would usually be shoved in goals by the team captain, only for them to yell at me when a goal went past me. "I told you I was bad in goals!" Would be my response.

On a cold winter morning, the wind blowing against

my skinny bare chicken legs, the teacher caught me messing about, and not paying attention to him. I was in trouble.

For the purpose of storytelling, I'd love to detail what was said, but alas, I was not listening.

With an angry look in his eyes the PE teacher barked at me to run 10 laps of the pitch as punishment while the rest of the class played football. Sprinting off to do my laps, I realised that I actually preferred this, and made a conscious effort to double my efforts of clowning around in future classes so that I could be "punished" further.

It took a long time for me to discover my passion. I always felt like a bit of an odd one out. My first taster of what was to come arrived when I was around 15 years old; some of the kids as a prank, decided it would be completely hilarious to fill my school back pack up with rocks and bricks.

To their dismay, I saw it as a challenge, acting like I didn't notice as I picked the back pack up – the straps struggling under the load. I kept the rocks in my pack all week, walking home with it each day, despite the damage it was doing to my school books (and my spine, as I was told).

During this time, I established an even greater lack of interest in sports and absolute disdain for any kind of organised extra-curricular activity. I began finding any excuse to bunk off my P.E. class; "Left my trainers at home Sir!" or, "Forgot my kit today," and, "bad ankle Sir!"

Sometime between the ages of 10-15 years, as an impressionable young man, I distinctly remember reading an article in the local newspaper about a lad from the area who had completed the super tough Royal Marines training and had been awarded his Green Beret. The story described how the Royal Marines underwent the longest and hardest military training in the world and only the fittest and the toughest could make it. Their symbol – a simple Commando Dagger emblazoned on the side of their sleeve was like a beacon for me. This was the seed which sowed in my mind, dormant for many years.

As my older teenage years were spent spectacularly flying off my skateboard, downing straight bottles of brandy (not recommended), playing guitar terribly in a punk band and meeting up with my friends to whoop them on "Halo: Combat Evolved" …. My younger years were spent in the park playing armies with toy guns.

My brother and I would play soldiers in the woods and on the surface, it was just a game. However, in my mind I was already there. While we would run around, our gazes fixed through the flimsy plastic scopes on our fun-size firearms, I would imagine myself wading through rivers, the slimy water submerging my legs. The beads of sweat seeping down my dark green face, plastered with camouflage paint, as I stealthily negotiated hostile territory on some secret mission in the dense, humid jungle.

I said previously I was not blessed with any skills. But I soon realised that if I completely focussed my attention and all my effort to something that I was really interested in, I could blow it out of the water.

During my high school years I certainly was not blessed with good looks or with much confidence. Huge red spots littered my face for years, leaving deep pitting and scars. I was to receive a now banned treatment, that in a bid to clear me of my acne made my skin peel off. It flaked away into a pile of dead, dry skin on my desk. But the acne remained unscathed.

Years and years of hospital visits to see doctors, dermatologists, laser surgeons and plastic surgeons all remained fruitless. The spots were too deeply embedded into my skin and they were not going away.

To make myself feel a bit better about myself, I began lifting weights. Not real weights, I would fill up old juice bottles with water to create make shift dumbbells and perform bicep curls and press ups in my bedroom. My mum encouraged me to go circuit training with her at the local leisure centre and I enjoyed training and seeing the results it was beginning to have on my body. While we only went once a week, it was something I enjoyed.

During my final year in high school, Summer was in full swing and school sports day was rapidly approaching. As mentioned previously I had absolutely no interest in organised activities, so during a team meeting I made zero input and kept myself quiet in the corner. I was never the fastest runner, had very little skill, so I was not expecting to be picked for any events, nor did I particularly want to be.

As expected, the athletic boys and girls were all up for taking part and the same small group of athletes were picked to participate in the events. The teachers, observing this, quickly made a rule stating that individuals are only allowed to participate in a maximum of 2 events. This meant a change in strategy and left a few events with no contenders. Namely, the 400 metres and the relay. Referencing the 400 metres, the team captain suggested, "Max can do it."

Whether he saw some potential in me or I was just the first person that came to mind who wasn't slow, I do not know. But I agreed to run this race, plus the relay. It was all set.

Sports Day arrived; it was a lush warm sunny day with a slight breeze. In the UK, we don't get many days like this anymore. The main events were run - the 100m,

200m and all that was left was the 400m and the relay.

The call came for the 400m runners to get ready. We formed up on the track and walked our way into our starting positions. I was in the outside lane. I felt isolated from everyone and could not see any of the other runners as they were all behind me. I had no strategy. Adrenaline coursed through my veins and my heart rate accelerated. I composed myself and focussed my thoughts, awaiting the starting gun. I was just going to have to run as fast as I could, for as long as I could. I didn't want to let the side down.

A loud bang erupted as the starting gun broke the tense silence. I bolted. Pumping my arms and driving my legs, slamming my heels down violently into the floor to propel myself forwards with my toes. I reached top speed as the track began to bend. I kept focussing my gaze directly in front of me, following the curve of the track. I kept waiting to see the other runners. "Any second now, and they'll be there to my left," I told myself, "Then just keep up with them."

I was running as fast as I could and I just kept pushing, kept breathing, maximum effort. The lactic acid built up, my muscles hurt and my heart pounded. I was not going to stop or slow down. I hit the final bend without slowing, all that was left was the final straight. Still no runners to my left. I maintained the pace and pelted over the finish line in first place. Not only winning the race by far, but also achieving a sports day record.

This was when I realised that even though I was not the fittest or the fastest, if I pushed myself and did not give in to the overwhelming desire to stop then I could be successful in whatever I was trying to achieve.

In 2004, I was dossing around between different college courses and working full time in the kitchen of a restaurant. At the time, the advert for the Royal Marines seemed to be absolutely everywhere. Billboards, TV and in Magazines. Whenever I took a trip to cinema, there it was; "99.99% Need Not Apply". They'd tell me not to bother filling out the application form. It beckoned me. I wanted the challenge, I wanted to be part of something elite. I applied, went through the recruitment process, worked on my fitness and eventually attended the Potential Royal Marines Course. The PRMC was the final hurdle to beginning recruit training. A three-day selection test of non-stop physicality, they had high standards and the course had an equally high dropout rate.

Back in those days, we knew very little about what this course entailed. We would get appointment slots at the Armed Forces Careers office, and while we were waiting to be seen by an advisor an old VHS video cassette would play on a TV in the corner. The screen would depict guys in military fatigues, khaki bottoms and boots covered head to toe in mud running around, jumping over obstacles and climbing along ropes. I remember speaking with a couple of guys who had recently attended the PRMC and had failed, they were in the Careers Office trying to organise a second and final attempt.

I would hear rumours of the so-called "bottom field" and how the warm up before the assault course would go on forever and guys would just be forced to quit. I was told that press ups and pull ups were done "the hard way," but with no actual explanation of what this meant. The only advice I received, from a failed candidate was "whatever you do… just don't stop."

In January 2005, my time would come. I was on the train to Lympstone Commando where I would spend the next 3 days experiencing life in the Royal Marines. Concurrently, the Royal Marines would be looking at me closely, to see if I was a suitable candidate.

These three days would push me further outside my physical comfort zone than I had ever experienced before. We were greeted outside the gym by a Physical Training Instructor (PTI), who was quite possibly the buffest guy I had ever met in my life at this point. It was explained, that our T-shirts had to be tucked in at all times during the PRMC, so that those who were to be sick would have to do it inside their tops. This meant that it wouldn't make a mess on the floor, and they wouldn't be able to stop.

Over the next 2 days, we were tested in the gym, running in the lanes and the dreaded "bottom field". The bottom field followed by the assault course caused a few drop outs due to sprained ankles and dislocated shoulders. We would try and rest during the night to recover for the next day, but being woken up at 5am to run around a courtyard, being held in stress positions and doing press ups for seemingly forever did not help.

The test that caught me out most was Gym Test 2. This was described as "a series of individual and team stances to test you physically and mentally." Sounded easy enough. The PTI in this one however, was the angriest and scariest man I had ever met in my life.

There were around 45 of us on the course. We were all stood to attention in 3 neat ranks outside the gym while the PTI gave us our brief. We were told that we were not allowed to giggle, talk, fart, scratch or even wipe the sweat off our face whilst we were in the gym. T-shirts were to be tucked in tightly, so that if we were sick, we could do so down our top and not make a mess on the gym floor.

What started off as a gradual warm up, quickly accelerated to a full-on session at maximum intensity. We were not allowed to stand still. Not allowed to itch, fidget or even wipe the sweat off our brow, our focus was on performing every exercise at lightning speed. We had to sprint everywhere, perform a series of small circuit sessions at 100% effort, hurling ourselves along wooden beams, performing sprints, single leg bounds, medicine ball throws, sled pulls and even more sprints. We were being watched from all angles, if we didn't give 100%, we were told, we would not be successful.

Our "rest" position between sets of circuits and sprints, was to double mark time – a high knees sprint of 100% effort on the spot. Our knees were never high enough and we were never going fast enough. The PTI was in my face like a frenzied rottweiler, screaming at me to go faster, harder, higher. Nothing I did was good enough for him. As I was about to black out, the session ended. I was left gasping for air, barely able to hold myself up for the stretches.

While the PRMC was tough, I was successful. Being awarded a T-Shirt at the end that stated "Potential 0.01%" was a very proud moment for me. A PTI had told me 1000 other applicants had failed to get to the position we were going to be in. Other than a couple of races in school I'd never really won much in the past. I wasn't a confident kid, but this made me feel good. I went home, quit my job and doubled up on my training.

Much of 2005 was then spent at the Commando

Training Centre Royal Marines. It was a tough year with many highs and lows, but it was also one of the best years of my life. I had grown up without a father and the Royal Marines provided a series of male role models for me to look up to. Life just felt magical at this time, I was outdoors a lot, I met new people, made new friends, was fitter than ever, experienced so many different things and learnt so much.

I completed the 33 weeks of Commando training as an "Original" Troop member. What this means is that you stay with the original troop you joined and complete training with them. A lot of people get injured or fail certain parts of the course and they get pushed back to re-do parts of training with another troop.

I would serve until May 2009, seeing active service on Operation Telic (Iraq) three times. After I left, there were some tough years ahead. It was a long road filled with many life challenges and obstacles. It took a long time, but eventually I got to where I wanted to be; which was working as a security operative. I had a great time working in security, in the UK, Europe and also maritime anti-piracy, where I made some lifelong friends.

In 2014 I decided the security industry was no longer for me and began working in fitness, as well as doing some security jobs, until eventually I stopped doing security. The money wasn't quite what was I was used to with security so I ended up working for the Police as a Control Room Operator, a job I enjoyed for about 4 years, and again made some great friends. Then I switched back to working in fitness and I remain doing that to this day, although I have certainly branched out in the field rather than just doing gym shifts here and there and group exercise sessions in the park, like when I started.

Now as a Fitness Enthusiast, I make YouTube videos where I give fitness advice and attempt to document some of my training and physical challenges.

My aim now is to try and enjoy my life as best I can, explore my passions, keep training hard and give myself little goals along the way.

I wanted to compile my thoughts and memories regarding some of my favourite challenges and adventures over the last couple of years. This book is written in my own words, while I am not a professional author or accomplished writer – I want to tell my story of some of my most proud accomplishments and physical efforts. This book will also serve as a record of many of my youthful pastimes for me to dwell on when I am old and decrepit.

Between 2019-2021, I completed a few charity events and received some amazing compliments from many people, but I want to highlight that I am not some kind of superhero and I do not possess special abilities. I do not have a large sponsor or a huge budget to throw into making these challenges possible. I am just a normal man, working full time who has a passion for extreme physical adventure, a solid work ethic and a certain level of stubbornness.

While the hard physical effort was undertaken by me, I recognise that a lot of these adventures would not have been possible without the help of my friends, for whom I am eternally grateful.

My aim was always to spend as little money as possible in completing these challenges correctly, safely with consideration to the environment and other people – whilst maximising the amount of money I can raise for my chosen charities.

Whilst I am talking about my own physical accomplishments this book isn't me trying to showboat or say how good I am. I am not here racing anyone or trying to set world records. I recognise and believe that the only person I am challenging and competing against is myself. The journey often has a more lasting impact on an individual than the actual result.

Each chapter will be presented as a short story, that can be read in isolation or as part of a longer journey; from my lowest moments to some of my very best. I will also include some of my training theories and principles that I have relied upon over the years to increase strength and fitness. These principles have been fairly consistent regardless of the goal and been forged through decades of training, hard work, study, trial and error.

I believe that everyone on this planet has the ability to achieve things that are great. Whether through physical challenges, sport, arts, business or any other accomplishment – we are all individuals with our own unique interests. I believe that everyone has a story. This is mine.

Military Service

A timeline of my military service and a couple of short stories

Military Service

Royal Marines Commando

2005 Recruit Training
896 Troop Commando Training Centre Royal Marines

2005-2006 Operation Fardrum
R Squadron
Fleet Protection Group Royal Marines

2006 Operation Telic (Iraq)
539 Assault Squadron Royal Marines

2007 Operation Calash (Gulf of Aden)
Fleet Standby Rifle Troop RM Boarding Team
S Squadron / HMS Campbeltown

2007 Operation Telic (Iraq)
Fleet Standby Rifle Troop
S Squadron

2008 Operation Telic (Iraq – Persian Gulf)
FSRT RM Boarding Team
S Squadron / HMS Chatham

2008 Counter Piracy Troop
Fleet Protection Group Royal Marines

2009 Imperious Troop
Fleet Protection Group Royal Marines

Winter 2005
Commando Training Centre Royal Marines
The Commando Tests
Test 3: The Tarzan Assault Course

My legs felt like lead as I approached the water filled tank trap and leapt over it with all my power. My boots landed on the floor with a splash of water and I charged at the six foot wall - launching myself up, gripping on with my forearms and the rough brick dug into my skin. I thrust my hips up swung my legs up onto the top and quickly spun myself down onto the ground on the other side. The webbing and rifle, a combined weight of 31lbs slowed me down. The high aerial assault course had been tough, but I was now past the half way point and making good time.

I charged over the metal frame and sprinted the distance to the next obstacle, the cargo net. I crashed to the floor and crawled as quickly underneath as I could, belly close to the floor and my elbows grazed on the rough stone underneath. Another obstacle down.

I leapt to my feet and sprinted to the next obstacle, the monkey bars. I held onto the metal support frame, stepped up onto the rubber tyres on the side of the water tank and reached for the bar. My hands grasped onto the iced over, cold metal bar with an overhand grip. I released my right hand and confidently tried to swing between the bars. My kit was weighing me down, my hands were cold and wet, the bars were slippery and I couldn't swing and grip as confidently as I thought I could. I hung on with both hands and made it across another couple of rungs before I felt my grip going. I tried to make it across, released my right hand and as I was swinging to grip onto the next bar my left hand slipped and I fell into the cold water below.

A Sergeant told me to get out and do the obstacle again. This time however, I was soaked head to toe and weighed significantly more.

I climbed out of the water tank and tried again. I made it to rung number three, and fell in with a spectacular splash.

"Stop fucking around and try again!" The Sergeant bellowed, before warning, "this is your last fucking chance."

I climbed out again, I made it to rung number two and I just hung there, clinging on desperate not to fall off, but my hands didn't have any strength left in them.

I lost my grip and plunged into the icy water for the final time.

"Get out," the Sergeant shook his head, "get out and fuck off."

He gestured behind him for me to head in the direction of the starting point. I started doubling, a defeated shuffle. I had failed the Commando Tests on the last but one day.

"Fucking pathetic," I heard the Sergeant from behind me mutter, as my dreams were shattered.

Angry and annoyed with myself, I forced the tear away from my eye and held my head up. A couple of my fellow recruits saw me approaching them and asked me what happened. They could see by my face something wasn't right.

"I fucked up," my face grimaced, "fell off those fucking monkey bars."

The lads, knowing how disappointed I was, took my webbing off me; offering to clean and dry it for me so that I could sort myself out.

I would be allowed one more attempt at the Tarzan Assault Course later that day. If I messed this up, then I was out. After 32 weeks of arduous commando training, I should have been ready. I was ready, but I had messed up.

It was only about 3 hours I had to wait for my test re-run, but it felt like an eternity. I had cleaned my rifle, showered, changed into clean clothes and scrubbed my boots. My webbing had been brushed down by my friends and was hanging up in the drying room.

After lunch in the galley the rest of the recruit troop had lectures to attend. I on the other hand, had to wait for my re-run time.

I sat alone in Jim's Diner and guzzled on bottle after bottle of Lucozade sport. This was the week of the Commando Tests. It was a tough week, and yet here I was on day 3; I'd already done the Endurance Course twice, the 9 Mile Speed March once and was now preparing to try the Tarzan Course for the second time. Having cramped up during my second Endurance Course run, I wasn't leaving anything to chance. I hoped the sports drinks would help rehydrate me and prevent any drops in performance.

My mind raced asking questions – how had I failed this? The monkey bars of all things! It's a rubbish excuse but, having warmed up for the Tarzan Course I was towards the back of the stack to begin. This is because there is a Tarzan Acquaint conducted a week or so prior and recruit's times are jotted down and then the starting order for the actual test are based on the scores from the acquaint; the faster times starting first. I unfortunately had diarrhoea at the time of this acquaint and was placed in quarantine for 48 hours; therefore didn't have a time from the acquaint and had to start last.

The troop had been warmed up and then put in a line based on times and then set off every couple of minutes. This meant I had been stood still for over an hour, watching the rest of the guys in my troop slide down the death slide and attack the course, and then come back chuffed to bits that they had passed. It was a freezing cold December morning, and my hands were completely numb. A weak excuse I know, but that combined with what was the hardest test for me, and some slippery bars had caused me to fail.

The Tarzan is a high aerial obstacle course that looms over the bottom field at Lympstone Commando. It begins with a climb up a tower that is approximately 40ft tall to begin the first obstacle aptly named "the death slide."

The recruit must hold onto a small piece of rope over a long rope that starts over head in the tower and proceeds down to the ground, 100ft or so in length. After the recruit successfully lands on the ground the hand held rope is thrown to the ground and the recruit then sprints off to begin the next obstacle. This rope is then dipped in a bucket of water to prevent it from catching fire due to the friction, and is then passed onto another recruit who is ready to start to the test. The course consists of 23 different obstacles that consist of varying different heights. The main Tarzan rope state stage is undertaken up to 30ft off the ground and at the time had no safety nets. (Due to some life changing injuries this has now changed). It then proceeds gradually towards ground level and then a sprint to the bottom field to tackle the obstacles there, including a 6ft wall, monkey bars, a chasm, a 12ft wall and then a final 150m dash to the final obstacle – the 30ft wall. In total it is around 1.5km in length and must be completed in under 13 minutes carrying a rifle and webbing (total weight of 31lbs).

It was soon approaching my time to re-take the test. I was determined to pass this time. Two of the other recruits had snuck down during lunch time with a towel to dry any water off the monkey bar rungs to prevent ice forming on the bars to give me less chance of slipping off again. I got rigged up, and doubled my way down to the starting point of the course.

After a brief warm up, I climbed to the top of the tower. I felt sick. This time there was no queue to delay the inevitable. I launched myself from the tower and smashed my way into the high rope section.

There are specific techniques required to undertake each obstacle. They are all unique and range from simply climbing a ladder, to swinging from ropes, running over planks of wood suspended in the air and making a jump, to climbing along ropes.

Once this was completed, I resumed with the rest of the course. There was a bit of a run to the tunnels and then the 12ft wall. What I found funny about this, was that most of the high rope course felt like it was working the upper body. But now it was time to run and my legs felt heavy and my sprint looked more like a jog. Still, I gave it 100% leapt off the 12ft wall and down the slight incline to the tank trap.

I knew these obstacles like the back of my hand. This section of the course is performed almost daily during the Battle Physical Fitness training stage in recruit training.

For the second time that day, I flew over the 6ft wall. The monkey bars were rapidly approaching. It was time to focus. I knew that I could complete this test, I just needed to get over those damn monkey bars. I'd done them countless time before.

As I approached the bars, I changed tactic. Usually, I'd try and swing two bars at a time. This time, I was going to slow it down and take it one bar at a time.

I gripped on, focussed and did not let the bars defeat me.

Monkey bars completed. I moved onto the next obstacle – I ran up the ladder and onto the 6 foot wall that zigzagged, reached the end of the wall and jumped off with a 2 footed landing.

The next obstacle was the chasm. It's basically a rope that goes horizontally between two platforms, approximately 12ft off the ground. Part of the test is to crawl along half way and then fall off the rope, catching yourself and complete what is called a half regain.

I had previously struggled with regains earlier on in training, so this to me was a bit of a mental stumbling block. The last hurdle for me to complete before hitting the other obstacles that I knew I could do.

I pulled myself horizontally along the rope, my body balancing on the top of it above the chasm. I approached the half way point and dropped underneath the rope. I violently flipped myself back up and onto the top of the rope with so much force and ease I surprised myself. There was a Corporal watching who was offering me encouragement and he was extremely pleased at my effort. In my excitement, I shuffled forwards with my hand another inch or two and lost my balance and fell off the rope again.

"You're only supposed to do 1 regain!!" the Corporal shouted!

I performed another regain, and steadied myself on the rope. I continued with the rest of the course and approached the 30ft wall.

Powering up with all my reserves, I reached the top, gasping for air and blasted out

"Glover, Staff!"

To announce that I had finished.

"Pass," the Corporal announced, "just…"

Summer 2006
Iraq
Midnight

The rotor blades of the helicopter whirred to life, scattering dust up into the dry hot night. The black mechanical beast vibrated heavily and with a judder, we were airborne.

Under the cover of darkness, two Merlin helicopters left the UK military base at Basra Airport. Onboard, sat in silence were 15 Royal Marines Commandos. Their destination – The Maysan Province, some 150km away.

My eyes soon adjusted to the darkness. I glanced around at the other men in my section. Everyone was focused. It was pointless to try and talk, the noise of the helicopter drowned out anything but a shout as it skimmed over the Iraqi desert.

This was my first proper mission in an operational environment. I was 19 years old, nervous and excited at the same time. I exchanged a pensive smile with one of my brothers sat opposite me. It was his first mission too.

Heading North from the dry desert outside of Basra, we flew over the swampy region of Maysan in the darkness below. The province bordered Iran and was home to a population of Marsh Arabs. This population had suffered greatly during the decade prior; after Saddam Hussein (former President of Iraq) had constructed the Glory Canal; Water was intentionally diverted from the Tigris River as an act of punishment for an attempted uprising; an uprising encouraged by the then US President George H. W. Bush in 1991. This diversion of water effectively dried out the marshes and turned the wetlands into a scorching desert, resulting in a humanitarian and environmental disaster in the region. This was among a series of other reprisals that included mass executions, detention centres and reports of poisonous gas being used on villages.

Since the fall of Saddam in 2003, the water had begun trickling back into the area and the marshland started its slow recovery. We were going to be landing in an unfamiliar area, complete with swamps and lakes juxtaposed by a dusty desert; containing a population of Marsh Arabs who lacked trust in coalition forces; who, after encouraging their uprising went on to pursue a policy of non-intervention while the subsequent bloodletting from Saddam's troops began.

Attacks on Coalition Forces had intensified in recent weeks. British Forces were bogged down in the southern city of Basra; achieving nothing except serving as target practise for a determined insurgency. They were hitting us hard, several times per day with increasingly larger rockets, mortars and more sophisticated improvised explosive devices that Western forces had ever encountered.

As we neared the landing site our primary mission remained in my mind: To covertly insert, gather intelligence and disrupt the supply chain of insurgent firepower and deter the enemy from further attacks on coalition forces in the city centre. Our secondary mission was to liaise with, and equip the local Coast Guard, who were currently sitting around doing nothing; allowing the insurgents to operate in the area with impunity.

As the Merlin glided through the night sky, a brilliant flash of light erupted from inside the aircraft and sliced through my thoughts. I glimpsed to my left as the RAF crewman angrily reprimanded one of the Marines for taking a sneaky photo on his wind up camera. Through the darkness I could see the shine of white teeth of all the Commandos around me chuckling like naughty school boys as he potentially gave our position away.

We were squished together like sardines. My body armour and webbing wedged me into my seat with my back to the starboard side of the aircraft, securely fastened in by the worlds most complicated seat belt. I had my trusty General Purpose Machine Gun placed carefully on the deck at my feet, six hundred rounds of ammunition, 24 hours of rations, my personal cleaning kit, weapon maintenance equipment, a large knife and

2 litres of water packed neatly into pouches around my hips. The rest of my ammo, water, food and equipment was firmly stowed away in my bergen (military rucksack) that was waiting patiently for me a few feet away.

"FIVE MINUTES!" The Corporal shouted and held up his hand to gesture the number Five.

The same message and gestures were passed on by each man down towards the rear of the aircraft. Until we were all updated and sat silent again.

My heart rate picked up. The RAF Merlin began the descent.

"ONE MINUTE!" Bellowed the Corporal.

We were going to be landing in the middle of nowhere on a small track with a swamp either side of it. To top it off, it was going to be pitch black.

We had studied the landing site intensely with satellite imagery, aerial photography and maps during the day. We had to have faith that the pilot knew what he was doing and that we would be exiting the helicopter onto solid ground, and not the serpent infested water.

The Merlin swooped to the side and rapidly began screeching to the ground. I felt it decelerate sharply until it swiftly hovered in place and touched down with a thud.

The moment the wheels hit the deck was our cue. Point Man, brandishing a Light Machine Gun sprinted off the rear exit ramp into the darkness. I was number 2 and followed hot on his heels, gripping my machine gun by the carrying handle and running off the metal ramp at speed. I threw the sling over my shoulder, my boots struck the dusty, but firm track and I ran at full pelt. My heavy kit suddenly felt weightless as the adrenaline kicked in.

I could barely see anything except the back of the Marine in front of me. I ran as fast as I could so that he wouldn't vanish into the darkness. In front of me, the powerful whoosh of the rear rotor blades spun at hundreds of rotations per minute blasting air that felt like a tornado hitting my face. We veered slightly to the right to avoid being split in half by the sharp metal blades and continued at pace for about 100 metres where we began to establish a secure perimeter. I quickly deployed the bipod legs and placed my GPMG on the floor, pushing the carrying handle to the side and violently dropped to the prone position. My elbows scraped into the dust and I grasped the trigger mechanism grip with my right hand; placed my left hand over the stock and tightly pressed my shoulder into the wooden butt. The bipod legs tilted forward as I looked down the long barrel of my machine gun. We lay stationary staring out towards the dark track to secure the area and establish all round defence while the rest of the troops were inserted.

The sound of boots thudding on the track from the rear towards me was quickly followed by the reassuring sounds of fellow Marines crashing down into a defensive fire position to my left and right.

A few seconds passed and the dust, kicked from the downdraft of the helicopter began to envelope me as the Merlin rocketed off.

The sand and small rocks lashed my exposed neck below my helmet, stinging like an army of ants biting my skin. I maintained my gaze, focussed on the defensive arc to my front. As the helicopter rose into the night sky and moved to an overwatch position, the chudder faded slightly and there was a slight respite as the lashing of the sand stopped. The air was still.

Seconds later, the second Merlin screamed into position, pelting me with more dust and sand as the pilot carefully tried to position our boats underslung in a cargo net onto the track in total darkness.

This took a little bit longer than we had liked. It required the pilot a few attempts to manoeuvre into position and each time he did we were covered in a layer of sand that got inside all of my pouches, pockets, ears, nose and most annoyingly… inside my machine gun.

I tried to shield my weapon to prevent any obstruction

of the working parts.

Fuck, that's going to be a bitch to clean.

The pilot released the underslung load and rapidly ascended, joining the other Merlin and both left the area at full speed. Their rotor blades slowly disappearing into the distance.

We lay still and silent in the darkness, alert, watching our arcs.

As the chopping of the helicopters faded, they were replaced by the eerie howling of what sounded like hundreds of wild dogs who had been disturbed by the commotion. Like a pack of werewolves, they howled around us seemingly from all directions. The haunting sound pierced the still, muggy air for about ten minutes, before they too, were eventually silent.

Between six of us, we shared a night vision monocular. We passed it around so that we could see our surroundings clearer. After a few more minutes in all-round defence were began to get on with our mission.

We were dropped off approximately 1km from our laying up position. The reason for this, was because we were only allocated two helicopters for the mission, but we needed three. One of the Merlins was heading back to Basra Airport to refuel, and then was due to return with another load of Marines, a journey of over 300km that would take some time.

Intelligence had indicated that the insurgents could rain down a barrage of rockets and mortars (Indirect Fire - IDF) on our location within thirty minutes of them establishing our position. We were hoping to get in undetected, however a helicopter can be heard from some distance away. We had already been in position for fifteen minutes so we had to leave the area fast.

Our task now was to lift and shift all our equipment swiftly and stealthily to a temporary harbour position 1km away; liaise with a small, long range Army patrol who were already out on the ground; prep and pump the boats up; and then wait for the remainder of the troops to arrive before we could disappear into the water.

It was not our preferable insertion method; we had discussed pumping the boats up at base and then being dropped by the chopper into the water. The powers that be, in all their wisdom told us this would not be happening. So, troops were shuttled in and a hard hike before we could get in the water it was. Not ideal, but it was the hand we were dealt with.

We had to proceed on foot carrying not only our personal kit (which in my case weighed over 85kg) but also the six Zodiac inflatable boats, engines (each Zodiac complete with engine weighed over 120kg), hundreds of litres of fuel and not forgetting the cargo net itself which would need to be returned to the RAF.

Not only did we have to shift all this kit, we had to do so in the dark, wearing body armour and helmet, in 35 degrees heat, quickly and quietly; whilst remaining alert and maintaining a defensive posture. This sounds like a daunting task, but we were Her Majesty's Royal Marines Commandos, and we had a job to do.

With some assistance, I hauled my bergen onto my back and grabbed an engine and lugged it as far as I could. I placed it down on the floor and another Marine took over while I shook my arms out. We leap frogged like this into the dark night.

After some time, we took a quick rest stop to survey our surroundings. Sweat was dripping off my head. The inside of my helmet felt like a swamp and my long sleeve desert camouflage shirt, layered with sand, stuck to my arms.

Up ahead, approximately 200 metres away, we were aware that there was a cross roads between tracks. I held the night vision monocular up to my eyes and the track was illuminated for me in brilliant green. I could make out a stationary British Army WMIK sat in darkness. A unique and familiar sight to me from SAS books and films, the open top Land Rover was heavily armed with a machine gun similar to my own, a spare rugged tyre mounted to the side and stacks of jerry cans piled up in the rear, visible through the roll bar cage.

My section remained stationary in vigilant all-round defence, while one of the Corporals and a Marine made their way over to the WMIK to make themselves known as friendlies.

The WMIK backed up and the squaddies offered their assistance in ferrying some of the boat kit the rest of the way. While we patrolled on foot to the side and rear of the vehicle carrying our personal kit plus the odd engine that wouldn't fit on the Land Rover.

We arrived at the Harbour Position, and quickly began assembling our boats. The Army patrol assisted with security and then departed into the night. For this operation, they would be covering the ground, and we would be on the water.

Each Zodiac boat had to be pumped up in sections, a metal floor plate attached inside and then the engine and fuel hoses needed to be connected. This was not a leisurely trip to the beach. We had to be efficient and therefore had rehearsed this for hours and hours back in the airport base; much to the amusement of onlooking Royal Engineers who wondered why we were messing around with blow up boats in the middle of the desert.

With the boats assembled and positioned in cover by the waters edge ready to deploy; we secured the landing site and lay in position, awaiting the return of the RAF Merlin so we could begin with our mission.

Lessons

The Importance of Pride

In the face of a seemingly difficult insertion and one that was not our preferred method; we were undeterred in our approach. Royal Marines have a proud history, and have proven themselves in battles all over the world against the odds. When faced with the challenge, we did not complain, whinge or hesitate. We got on with it, completed the task and moved on.

Spread the Load

A bit off subject here – I have always been fascinated by insects, particularly ants. I enjoy watching them scurrying around about their business.

Often, they will be seen carrying grains of sand or soil to build their colonies. I have sat back previously and studied an ant's colony being built over a period of days and was amazed about the sheer volume of sand they were able to shift. They had built a relative mountain!

We could learn something from ants. These tiny little

workers operate as a team; ferrying the small grains from Point A to B efficiently, one grain at a time. This is exactly what we did to complete our insertion, and we worked together in a leap frog fashion as efficiently and as quickly as we could to complete the task.

Don't Be Afraid to Ask for Help

Royal Marines and their Army counterparts are always keen to get one up on the other. During operations however, we recognise that we are all part of the same team and the interservice rivalry is forgotten (until we're back at the base!). Our Army colleagues were more than happy to offer their support during our insertion and we were more than happy to accept their help. Rivalry and pride should never get in the way of the mission. Being competitive is good to maintain standards, but it is very important that it is not to the detriment of the task. This is something I have seen many a colleague, manager and supervisor in my civilian jobs fall foul to. Rather than play their team in positions to suit their ability, they preferred to make others look bad, to make themselves look seemingly better or just mess people around in some daft power play.

New Beginnings

New Beginnings

I left the Royal Marines in 2009 an absolute shell of a man. Smoking 40+ cigarettes a day, I had a very unhealthy relationship with alcohol. I am quite an extreme person. I am not passionate about many things, but if I am into something I take it to the extreme. Go all in. Back in those days I partied and drank hard, putting everything into it.

This led to me being in a serious amount of debt that quickly spiralled out of control once I left the safety net of the Royal Marines. Refusing to adapt and burying my head in the sand, I tried to maintain the same lifestyle I had as a young Marine. A lifestyle where I had found myself able to get drunk every night.

This was not sustainable, but the damage had already been done. I was staying at my mums and I am ashamed to say, unable to contribute much at the time towards the household expenses. My mobile phone was frequently cut off by the service provider because I couldn't pay the bill. I couldn't afford a car. I'd take pay day loans out to keep my previous creditors at bay, and would borrow money from anywhere I could to go out drinking.

Despite this, I always worked hard and after leaving the Marines I had quickly got a job as a night porter in a hotel. Unfortunately, the salary was not enough and the debt spiral got so out of hand that my monthly wages were not even close to covering my debt payments, let alone paying for food, or anything else. Needing extra cash, I applied for more jobs.

Within a few weeks I had a full-time night job, a full-time day job and a part time weekend job. In the day time I would work in the kitchen of a restaurant; washing dishes, mopping the floor and preparing food. I'd leave there in the evening to go to my night job in the hotel. Here, I'd be delivering room service, carrying people's bags to their rooms and assisting guests with anything and everything. Then on the weekends I was working in a school fitness centre. I was only sleeping two nights per week. It was tough, but this is what I needed to do to survive.

It was around this time that I decided I had to make some changes. I distinctly remember on one evening off I was in the local pub, pint in hand, cigarette in the other. I put my cigarette out and announced to whoever was listening that I was going to stop drinking, stop smoking and train for the half marathon. This gave me something to work towards. On top of this, I also decided to enter the Mr Wales competition that Summer. Even though I was working so many hours and sleeping so little, I would go for runs on my lunch breaks, perform dynamic tension exercises in work when no one was looking and do bodyweight exercises in between jobs.

After a couple of months, I entered a debt management programme. This made my out-of-control debt that little bit more manageable. This programme enabled me to leave one of my employments. I did not need to be working so many jobs and so I left the restaurant. This came at the right time, because I was totally exhausted. My fitness had been decimated by the poor life style choices I had made. Getting back into it was demoralising at first but I quickly improved.

As my training was going well and my health recovered, I decided to enter another race – the Men's Health Survival of the Fittest obstacle course. I'd stay nocturnal and go for night time runs, where I would do circuit training in the local park on the climbing frames. I couldn't afford a gym membership, and I certainly didn't need one.

I have some very fond memories of these park workouts. I'd teach myself calisthenics, and build the skills up. Sometimes at around 3am, a car would pull up in the car park. Local guys coming to smoke weed in their car. I'd see the spliff being lit as it would glow red from inside the cab of their car. I always wondered if they would see my silhouette in the darkness doing hand stands, planches and muscle ups on the climbing frames. I'd imagine them looking at their joint, then up at each other and saying, "That's some good shit!"

This was the start of my new beginning as a civilian. I kicked the alcohol addiction and poor lifestyle to the side, trained hard and achieved a time of 1:25 in the half marathon with only 3 months of training. I came 26th in the Men's Health Survival of the fittest. I didn't place very well in the Mr Wales contest, but I got on stage and gave it a go.

While I was still in loads of debt and hounded by problems, I had made my first steps towards a healthier path, and brighter future. A few years passed and I began working in private security and for a while, things went well.

Cardiff
Strippers

Cardiff Strippers

My head hit the desk, my long, greasy black hair cascaded onto my white shirt sleeves as my arms erected a wall between me and the rest of the class. The voice of the teacher droning on about a subject I really didn't care about echoed in the distance.

I sighed heavily and the dead skin that had fallen off my face blew across the desk, hit my sleeve and settled like a snow drift against my arm.

What had started as a few small spots years earlier had paved the way for mountains of large red boils on my face, volcanic white heads that left legions of painful sores deep under my skin.

Acne had ravaged my skin and just kept getting worse and worse. I had tried every spot lotion, ointment, soap, face wash and zit cream on the market. My mum had bought me a sun lamp and a facial steamer; all had proven ineffective – the spots just kept getting worse.

I had been advised to use the sun lamp for just a few minutes at a time, but when my bedroom door was closed, I would abuse it for an hour and a half in a desperate attempt to rid my face from the large red spots.

Eventually, the facial steamer was not enough for me either. My futile attempts saw me subjecting my face to longer and longer periods of steam. Then, duration wasn't enough for me; there wasn't enough steam or heat – it was too weak. I resorted to boiling a kettle and placing my face over the open lid and into the hot steam, closing my eyes and resisting the pain.

"To rid my face of these spots, it will be worth it," I told myself.

The acne just laughed at my attempts to fight it. Eventually, an appointment was booked with the doctor and I was prescribed medication that promised to rid me of acne in a few weeks.

I eagerly began taking the drugs, continued my regimen of washing my face ten times per day, scorching my skin with sun lamps and hot steam. The course of medication ended, and the acne remained unscathed.

After a review with the doctor, I was referred to a dermatologist at the hospital who was able to perform blood tests and prescribe stronger medication.

I was given a course of the strongest drug available. I was advised that there were potentially numerous side effects of this drug, including dry skin. I was told it was very aggressive and effective.

I began taking the drug immediately, and read through a long list of side effects associated with it. Within a few days I began to observe the aggressive nature of the drug and experienced a few of the side effects. My skin began to dry out, flake and peel off my face. At the end of an hour lesson in school my desk would be littered with dead and dry skin that had fallen off my face. The acne remained and my confidence that had already taken a beating hit an all-time low.

Kids would look at me as if I had some contagious disease. Red and purple mounds on my skin made my face resemble the planet Jupiter rather than the face of a 15-year-old boy.

I wouldn't say I was bullied in school, but my physical appearance around this time led to a barrage of comments that left me feeling like total shit.

Why don't you just pop them?

Don't you wash your face?

Just buy some Clearasil.

If only it was that simple. All of these kids with perfect skin looked great and couldn't comprehend. No one knew what I was going through, and I never told anyone.

I never tried to let any of this phase me, and put on a front. On certain days when it was particularly bad, I would hide my face on the desk, let the skin flake off onto the desk, then I'd discreetly brush it into my hand to dispose of.

Even though this was happening, and I felt a bit rubbish and extremely self-conscious, I tried to better myself in other ways. I lifted make-shift weights at home, did push ups and began to self-learn the guitar.

As my high school years came to a close and the exams approached, the spots had begun to dissipate naturally. I had been put on many courses of drugs and each time the dermatologist would review and suggest we keep going. I had been informed that the scars and deep pitting that would be left on my face after the spots finally left would be so bad that I would require plastic surgery to cover them up. They told me there was laser surgery options available, but they wouldn't work as the acne had been so severe and for so long.

The results of my training, combined with playing guitar meant I was very slowly gaining confidence and beginning to attract some attention from girls. For the first time in my life, I had girls talking to me who weren't looking disgusted when they did so.

The only trouble was, my self-confidence was so low I just thought they were taking the piss, or been put up to it as a joke by someone else.

These days it's cool to be different. People are a lot more accepting. When I was in school it was the opposite. It was cool to conform. If you stood out from the crowd you were "obviously gay," or people tried to beat you up or make fun of you.

When I finally found myself and stopped trying to be like everyone else was when my confidence began to creep up and I really started enjoying things.

I spiked my hair, starting skateboarding, created websites, formed a punk band and started drinking. When we went out, I'd drink more than anyone else. I'd have fun in my own way and had a great bunch of friends. Physically, I became bigger and stronger than most of the kids my age.

There are some simple lessons that I'd like to share from this stage of my journey:

- Find yourself and be yourself;

- When things are shit, keep your head up and keep smiling;

- Find ways to better yourself;

- Create a vision in your head of who you want to be and work towards it – but be patient as it can take time;

- Reassure yourself that things **will** get better.

Fast forward ten years….

I was dancing on stage in front of hundreds of screaming women. My hands reached up my body, gripping my vest at the neck and ripping it apart to reveal my bare, muscular torso. I was stood in the centre of a small group of male bodybuilders and models. Excited women had all paid £15 each to come and see us perform. We were Cardiff's answer to the Chippendales.

What had happened? How had a skinny high school kid, who lacked self-confidence; that was too ashamed to show his face in public; that had been told he would need plastic surgery to look normal; to an entertainer on stage, confidently showing off his body on stage in front of hundreds of women and stood alongside attractive men with some of the best physiques in the country?

The issue with my skin had resolved itself. While I had been put on the National Health Service waiting list for plastic surgery it was a very long time before I got to the top of that list. I can't imagine spotty teenagers are a priority for such a list.

By the time an appointment came through for me, I was in the Marines and having spent so much time outdoors and exercising over the years my skin had really begun to clear up. My skin, exposed to sunlight, a good diet and proper hydration showed only the remnants of the deepest scars and pitting. Even then, I was confident that they would not last forever. I looked in the mirror, it had been a hot summer in 2005 and my skin was a beautiful golden colour. I cancelled the appointment and let nature take its course. I didn't need plastic surgery.

After completing Recruit Training, I spent quite some time deployed in the Middle East and therefore saw a lot of sunshine; I had a permanent tan. I sweat a lot and I rarely wore sun cream. This is because when out on patrol in the heat of Iraq, the sweat would pore down my face, and the sun cream would go in my eyes. I needed my eyes to look for hidden improvised explosive devices and command wires in the dust. It was a judgement call I made at the time.

The sun clearly aged my skin, as I look a lot older than I actually am, but it removed any traces of the acne I had as a teenager.

That's how my skin improved, but what about my physique?

I hit the gym properly and started lifting weights in December 2005. This was during my time at Faslane. I got obsessed with the bench press and I began benching almost daily. Sometimes, when no one was about I would sneak off and do a few sets throughout the day.

During a brief time as part of a two-man QRF team, I noticed that there was a bench with some weights in the adjacent room. I'd be tooled up ready for action, and I'd go and do a few sets on the bench press. I liked the results and I enjoyed getting stronger. When I returned home after my first few months at Faslane, my mum asked me if I had been taking steroids!

I continued my fitness training throughout my time in the Marines. Lots of running, circuit training and weight training when I was able. I built a ripped physique and had a great colour. I was lucky in that I can walk past a window and get a tan and my skin turns a nice olive colour. I became a lot more confident with myself and during 2008 we landed on a Royal Navy warship for a week of training, only to discover that a photo of me taken in the Gulf by a Navy photographer was on the wall of the Wrens mess. I was now a pin up for the female sailors. The pinnacle moment of my career.

Upon leaving the Marines, and around about the time I started working in security, I restarted the weight training. I hit it with a vengeance. I was working mainly site security in the days / nights during the week, and then on the weekends I would do door work in the night clubs. On occasion, I would do the odd close protection gig.

Part of my motivation to train was because I worked with some big boys, and I didn't want to look small. My mentality at the time was the bigger you looked, the less likely anyone was going to mess with you. For me, this did seem to be true whilst working on the doors, but the complete opposite when on a night out.

I pumped iron hard, I would arrive at the gym with a 4-pint bottle of milk for me to chug immediately after my workout. I was focussed and determined.

After many months of working and grinding, I was invited to take part in some modelling work for charity. I did this and through that I was put in touch with the management of a new group that was being formed. I was still pretty skint at the time; I had built up a huge amount of debt before I left the Marines that needed paying off. Any opportunity to earn extra money was very welcome.

The idea was a one hour show of super buff men, entertaining women. It was supposed to be a lot classier than the typical male stripper gig and was being put together by women.

My invitation was for a day time meeting at a trendy bar in Cardiff. It was here that I would meet all of the other guys, the managers and the choreographer. Little did I know that it was not just a meeting but more of an assessment.

Whereas I was expecting us to sit down and have a coffee and talk about it, me and the guys were all stood in a line in front of the managers and the choreographer, music was played and the instruction to dance was given.

The guys to my left and right were both excellent freestyle dancers, they had rhythm and moved to the music and seemed to be enjoying themselves. I on the other hand, could not dance, had never enjoyed, could not feel "the beat" and had zero rhythm. I gave it a go, but I was stiff as a board and looked like an idiot. I felt so stupid and very nearly told them that this gig wasn't for me.

We were then given a few moves to learn and then we began to work on our first choreographed dance routine. It looked pretty daft. A group of muscular bodybuilders spinning around, trying to remember movements, getting it wrong most of the time and then collapsing in a heap huffing and puffing.

This continued on Saturdays for a few weeks, we got a little better but eventually we were told that the choreographer would no longer be working with us. I can only assume, that he was used to working with proper dancers, could see little hope in us and didn't want to put his name to our performance. The managers stepped in, telling us that they would be taking over the choreography.

For me, this was a lot better. It was structured, but we were not given complex dance routines to learn. We had a list of songs and certain moves we would have to do, usually together and the rest of the time we were free to do whatever we want. We were played to our strengths as well, so after the choreographed bits, I would be free to jump into the audience and get up close and personal with the ladies, pick them up in the air and throw them around a bit. Which was pretty much what I used to do on the dance floor anyway after a few vodka and Red Bulls, except this time I was wearing less clothes, and being paid.

I preferred this idea, but I was still struggling with the dance moves. I was given the sound track on CD and I would play it at home and rehearse the moves, I would play it in the car while I was driving and visualise the moves in my head. I started off rubbish, but with practice, practice and weekly rehearsals – I got better.

Eventually I could feel the beat and even when I was not dancing or practising, I could feel it wherever I went and music was played. I even found when I was in the gym I was walking in step to the beat. It felt weird, but like something had been unlocked.

The first show arrived and we absolutely killed it. It was a huge success and we continued with shows and private bookings. We had a great time and partied hard afterwards. It gave me even more motivation to train and look after my nutrition. My abs were chiselled and my skin was looking tight. I was very proud of my physique and the hard work that had got me there. We spend so much time in the gym, grinding and grafting and it was nice to actually get some financial reward for all of the effort.

Lessons

Perseverance

I absolutely sucked at this when I first started. I couldn't dance. I was even borrowing clothes off my friends because I was so skint leading up to it. But I practised and attended rehearsals. I knew that I was not as good as the others guys, but I wanted to be the best. I knew that I would have to train harder and for longer to be able to get to where I wanted to go. It took time, but eventually I got there. This was a fun time of my life, and I have some great memories.

The Company You Keep

There's countless quotes about how the company you keep determines what you become (or words to that effect). I was working with top physique athletes and they inspired me to better myself. Knowing that I was going to be stood next to them on stage and in photos, I did not want to look out of shape. They inspired me to work hard in the gym, we exchanged training tips and supported each other through the journey.

During a dinner we all had together, I confided with one of the bodybuilders that I was not happy with my legs in comparison to my upper body. He said:

"Just stop training upper body so much, and train legs

every time you are in the gym until they catch up,"

And he was right.

Remember to Have Fun

It's so easy to lose sight of this one. I look back and there was so much hard work, not only was I doing all of these rehearsals and training twice a day in the gym, I was also working 30+ 12 hour shifts a month in security! I was having so much fun with this adventure that I made time for it.

On top of having fun, I look back and see how far I had come. From the skinny, spotty school kid with no confidence, to being in the best shape of my life with groups of women paying to have their photograph taken next to me. I was dating more women than I had time for and even though I was still ducking and diving financially, I was happy and healthy.

One of the highlights for me at the time was when I was doing close protection security for a young male popstar. He was a bit of a heart throb for teenage girls. After his gig, small groups of fans were able to come back stage for a photo with him, a chat and an autograph.

As I stood in close proximity to the star while he spoke with the girls, a call came through on my radio ear piece from the venue management of a rather unusual request.

"We've got a group of the girls' mothers here," the bewildered voice said, "they're asking to be allowed back stage as well, but for a photo with the bodyguard!"

I passed this message on to the popstar who laughed, "why not?"

The women were ushered in and I posed for photos with them, a hilarious end to a great evening!

Taking a Chance

Taking a Chance

It was 2011, I was living a great life working in security, performing on stage, pumping iron, dating lots of women and partying hard.

I was still riddled with debt, but I was just about treading water. I was living in a small studio apartment in Cardiff Bay and I absolutely loved it.

That August however, in the space of one week I lost my job, my car and my apartment. To top it off, I had a speeding ticket and a parking fine for the same car that I had just lost. To say I was down in the dumps was an understatement.

I had one month to vacate my apartment and with no money coming in I was struggling. I was paying a lot of debts and I didn't have the financial resilience to go longer than a week or two without my income.

Luckily, my friend was an operations manager in a hotel. He got me an interview with the hotel he worked for and I was quickly in full time employment. However it was not a job I particularly enjoyed, I was working nights; the money wasn't great and didn't really pay the bills. But it was better than nothing and I am extremely grateful for it.

I remember mopping the floor at 4am wondering what the heck had just happened. I would have to move in with family to keep a roof over my head – something again which I am extremely grateful for.

Despite feeling tired and defeated, I still maintained my gym routine. Fortunately for me, a friend was a member of staff at the gym I trained so I was able to get a friends and family free membership.

I usually trained in the mornings after my night shift, but one particular day, I went to the gym in the evening.

It just so happened that at the same time there was a guy I knew from the Marines who was also training there. I hadn't seen him for a while, we got chatting and it transpired that he was working in Maritime Security. He gave me the heads up that there was soon to be some working going, and it paid quite well.

I went home and checked out the company he told me about. I had applied to countless maritime security companies shortly after I left the Marines and I never heard back from any of them. I sent this company my CV, but I certainly wasn't going to hold my breath.

The next day I received an email back from them, thanking me for my interest but telling me that I needed some maritime qualifications before they would consider my application.

I checked online for the specific course they mentioned I would need first (the rest could be done whilst working for them). It turned out the course cost £475 and I had approximately £500 to my name. I thought "fuck it," and rolled the dice.

I attended this course, threw everything into it, applied for several companies. I was offered an interview in Bournemouth; I was working night shifts in Cardiff at the time and attended this interview when I should have been sleeping. I received three lucrative job offers within the space of a week. I picked the one that was best for me and within 24 hours I received a deployment notice for the following day.

Things had suddenly moved very fast. I had no kit; I didn't even have a bag that would be suitable for deploying with! I didn't even know what to take. But first, I had to hand in my notice with my current employer. I felt bad letting them and my friend down. He understood, and I did it the right way. I attended the hotel during the day, spoke with the manager and explained the situation. They weren't pleased, but I was being offered my dream job which would see me flying to Mauritius in 24 hours-time and being paid a life changing wage.

I got all my stuff sorted, met up with my new team mates at Heathrow airport – who would become like brothers to me and as promised, within hours I was sat on a beach in Mauritius awaiting the start of my first deployment!

The Unthinking Moment

The Unthinking Moment

My knuckles turned white as I gripped onto the steering wheel. I rounded the corner with speed, narrowly missing the curb as I pushed my budget tyres to their absolute limits. Downshifting, the engine roared as I revved into second gear, shattering the silence of the dark, lonely night.

My foot slammed down on the clutch and with my left hand pushed the gear stick into third, carelessly releasing the clutch and driving my right foot onto the accelerator pedal until it hit the metal with a loud clunk.

Like a bat out of hell my dark coloured BMW gathered momentum. I hit 50mph as my car approached the straight. My foot stayed firmly depressed on the pedal, propelling the vehicle rapidly to speeds twice in excess of the legal limit. 60mph.

As the car red-lined, the engine squealed in protest, prompting me to change into fourth gear. My eyes welled up. The tears streamed down my cheeks. The street lights became a blur as I gazed at the end of the road ahead that was rapidly approaching. 70mph.

I'd lost my job, was financially broke, alone, had countless car problems I couldn't afford to get fixed, an injury that stopped me from training, I had fallen out with everyone close to me. Nowhere to live. Nowhere to go. No way out. I'd worked so hard my entire life, only to end up here. And this was the third time something like this had happened in as many years. My reality had become a nightmare of relentless and perpetual failure. No matter what I did, I'd always end up back here. A never-ending loop. I'd had enough, I didn't want to fight this battle any more. Break the cycle. I didn't want favours, handouts or anyone to feel sorry for me or help me back up onto my feet. I was going to end my life, tonight, on my own terms.

The final street light signified the end of the road. All that lay ahead was the empty black sky and a 90ft drop to the cold sea below. 80mph. This is it.

In what could have been my last final seconds on this earth, my mind began to visualise and transported me to my potential destination; I'd driven off the cliff in a suicide attempt. My mangled car shattered on the rocks, the wheels still spinning as the waves crashed over the wrecked metal. But I'd survived. And just like the car, my body was crumpled beyond repair. Paralysed for life.

As the car hurtled towards this possible future, I imagined the pain, the despair and I could feel the deep regret. This was the make-or-break moment. The sliding doors moved quickly and I slammed on the brakes as hard as I could and the car juddered side to side as it came to a dramatic halt just feet away from the cliff edge. I maintained my tight grip on the steering wheel, bowed my head and cried my eyes out.

In that unthinking moment, following an upsetting period in my life, my emotions had gotten the better of me. I focussed on all the things I didn't have, forgetting all the things I did have – my health, my family and my friends.

I have not shared this story with many people, nor have I ever particularly felt the need to talk about it. This happened during my mid-twenties and the stories written in this book would never have happened had I taken the other option that night.

I write this story in this book to hopefully serve as a reminder to anyone reading this that has found themselves in a similar situation; there is light even after the darkest of nights.

Lessons

Perspective
Things aren't always as bad as they seem. I let my emotions get the better of me my thoughts lacked any kind of rationality.

A Suicidologist once told me:

"Given the chance, life will find a way."

It was at the last second my mind projected an image of one of the possible outcomes of my action. An image of full body paralysis and my car totally destroyed. My situation felt bad, but I was missing the bigger picture. I still had a lot to live for which in that unthinking moment I had taken for granted.

Looking back, I had very selfish reasons for wanting to kill myself; perhaps I wanted to try and hurt those who had hurt me. Had I continued I certainly would have succeeded and the reality is that is not actually something I wanted.

A Resolution

This wasn't the first time I'd lost it and I'd suffered what one could call a mental health crisis. But I would say that this was one of the most serious incidents. I needed to find a resolution because this was not an ideal way for me to live. I developed a set of rules to help prevent me from spinning out of control:

- Stop drinking / drugs - When I drank regularly, I fucked things up, pissed people off and spent all of my money. I'd create unnecessary problems and put myself in a position where I was unable to deal with any problems I already had;

- Get Organised – When I was in the Marines, I had become institutionalised to an organised structure. We were given orders and just followed them. A list of timings and details would be left on the wall for us to adhere to. When I left the Marines, I missed having this structure. Not only that, I was living in a mess. I had stuff everywhere and nowhere to store my items. By organising my life – in terms of maintaining a structure to my living space, and also a planned structure to my day was very useful. I like my living space to be as clear of clutter as possible. Otherwise, I have found this leads to a cluttered mind, and pent-up frustration. It also makes it a lot easier to clean, which to me assists with this cycle;

- Create a Character – I believe that with the proliferation of social media, a lot of people have done this one; possibly without even realising it! I began to imagine my life as a movie; I was the director / producer / main character. I stopped watching TV. Why would I want to spend my time, my life watching other people live theirs? It was so much more fun when I could create my own scripts and do whatever I set my mind to. As the director of my movie – I would give myself all the best roles and scenes!

- Find a Direction / Purpose – This helped massively and works hand in hand with goal setting. From physical challenges to creating things like videos or writing books.

For me, this is not a definitive list and it certainly is a work in progress. But I thought I would share this with you as this book is also a self-evaluation.

The Triple
Challenge

Triple Challenge

I always had some bonkers ideas. I always wanted to try things, different things that most people would not consider normal. And being a typical introvert, it was often difficult to set these things up. Trying to explain to people that you want to jump into a pool to try and drown yourself, push against a moving car, swim across a freezing lake or have a full workout lifting people as weights, the question was always asked, "why do you want to do this?"

After much deliberation I found my gateway, my reason to be able to do these things. I would explain that I want to make a YouTube video and suddenly all of these doors opened. Now people I was speaking with to arrange these challenges were open to the idea and quite supportive. For some videos, I even received hundreds of applications from willing participants!

So that is how my channel started, eventually I started getting more and more views and now it is a second source of income for which I am very grateful. And while I am not a massive YouTuber by any means, this allows me to do things I enjoy or to put my creative ideas down and get something back for them.

To show my appreciation for the audience watching

my videos I try my best to give some exercise advice and answer questions, to give back to those who have supported me on my journey.

Sometime in 2019 I noticed that YouTube had launched a great tool for interacting with your subscribers (or so I thought at the time...) They enabled a community "post" option where you can post a photo, some text or a poll. I placed a poll for my viewers to vote on what challenge I should do next and here were the options:

1. 10-mile run (how the Parachute Regiment do it – carrying 45lbs of weight... this was by popular request in comments on my previous videos).

2. Carry 200lbs on my back up and down a mountain

3. Do 1000 Pull Ups

As I monitored the poll and saw the votes coming in became apparent that my subscribers wanted to see me run 10 miles carrying 45lbs... They must all know that it had been years since I last ran more than a few metres and clearly wanted a laugh at my expense. I put this down to being a former Royal Marine (over 10 years ago at time of the challenge) but despite this they wanted to see how a Bootneck would get on at the Parachute Regiments fitness test. They didn't seem fazed by the fact that I'd barely be able to pass the fitness test for the scouts let alone the test for one of the Army's toughest regiments.

So, I resigned myself to accept two hilariously fun hours of huffing and puffing for my subscribers' entertainment. When I checked the post hoping to see a surge of votes for one of the other challenges, I saw a comment from Kettlebells123456 suggesting I do all three back-to-back or over a 24-hour period. "Not a chance!" I thought to myself, had quite the chuckle and went about my day.

Fun Fact! One of my quirks: I am known to have epiphany moments whilst in the shower. So, there I was, lathering myself up with soap and washing myself down feeling the cool water on my skin when Mr. Kettlebells suggestion became the best idea since sliced bread.

Having made myself decent, I took to my YouTube channel, creating a live stream where I made my pledge. I accepted the challenge, committing to raise money for SSAFA the Armed Forces charity. I would do no training for this challenge and would undertake it at the earliest opportunity, which was in a few days time.

Most normal people who work full time on their days off may have a lie in, do something chilled or go and visit somewhere fancy. Not me. Nope my alarm went off like a gun shot at the crack of dawn and as I went about my morning routine – shower, breakfast, coffee and some more coffee.

With urgency I diligently began to piece my kit together to make the ideal weight for challenge 1 – the 10 Miler. To prove that I wasn't running this with a helium bergen I hurled my pack onto the balcony where I had set up my bathroom scales and got the camera out to show any trolls that I was indeed going to be running with the specified weight.

I'd spent a great deal of time the night before planning my 10-mile route and I downloaded the MapMyRun app to my phone as a way of tracking and timing my run.

All ready to go, I stepped out of my apartment into a cloudy morning. The temperature was perfect, neither too hot nor too cold and slight breeze to keep me cool.

Every other human being in the area was on the morning commute, coffee in hand, head down glued to their phone on auto pilot, zombie victims of their daily grind apocalypse. Juxtaposed by me an energiser bunny full of beans, rucksack on my back, GoPro in hand ready for action. Walking a few hundred metres, I broke into a gentle jog around the Cardiff Bay area.

This was one of the first times I had started a video challenge near to where I lived. Usually, it would involve a lot of prep, a lot of travel and a lot of time. This would be a piece of cake.

It had been a long time since I had done anything like this and I had decided to opt with the old way we used to do speed marches in the Royal Marines, which was to do a slow run on the flats and a fast pace walk on the hills. Albeit, my fitness was not quite what I had as a serving Royal Marine!

I was going strong and actually enjoying myself when I hit my first hurdle. The MapMyRun app had defaulted to kilometres and I was supposed to be running in miles. This completely threw me and I lost about 5-10 minutes around a quarter of the way through trying to figure out how to change the settings on the app. But it seemed that I was unable to do this while the app was tracking.

This is one of the things I absolutely detest about fitness these days. While these devices and apps are all well and good, sometimes we can spend so much time faffing about with them that we actually lose a considerable amount of productive training time.

Due to my inexperience of using MapMyRun app I stitched myself up and rather than closing the run down and then restarting I adopted a new strategy. This involved a lot of Google conversions when running to ensure that I was doing the correct distance and also trying to figure out my pacing!

While this was annoying – it was my first lesson of this challenge. Preparation. I had not prepared enough for this challenge. I should have familiarised myself with the app beforehand. Had I downloaded the app a few days prior, I could have taken it out for a trial run and discovered that it defaulted to kilometres and adjusted it.

I chugged away at a fairly decent pace, but alas, I had fallen behind my target time. My walking pace up hill was too slow and looking back I wish I had just run up the hills.

In a desperate bid to make up the time I began running as fast as I could for the last mile or two, however it was not good enough to complete in the target time and I achieved a finishing time of 2:03. Not quite up to the standard, but in hindsight it's not actually that bad considering I hadn't run for some time. That was my first run with weight in over 10 years. Challenge 1 Complete!

Slightly disappointed with this, but then I remembered that I hadn't trained at all for this and that finishing it and pushing myself out of my comfort zone was an achievement.

Returning home, I hydrated, had some chicken and rice and then filled my car boot up with dumbbells, weighing scales and water. I began the car journey up to the Brecon Beacons for stage 2 of the challenge.

The journey itself wasn't too bad, taking me about an hour to reach my destination. As I arrived, the car park was quite busy, full with avid hikers walking towards the popular mountain. Driving around the carpark a couple of times, unable to find a parking space I was cursing to myself that I'd have to start from further away. Then, a stroke of luck, a small hatchback pulled out leaving a tiny parking spot. With motoring skills that would be worthy of Top Gear I managed to manoeuvre my 5 series BMW into the miniscule space.

The next bit took a lot longer than planned. I was trying to sort my kit out to weigh exactly 200lbs, but the rucksack I was using at the time was a medium sized civilian pack. Whilst it was lovely and comfortable it wasn't really suitable for carrying lots of kit.

Normally when I go up the mountains I overpack for any eventuality I can think of. Warm kit, first aid kit, flasks of coffee, cookers, waterproofs, emergency rations, cyalume snap lights, emergency shelters etc. But in order for me to fit the number of dumbbells required I actually had to ditch some of this kit. Mainly the warm kit, which I was to later regret.

Trying to weigh this pack to get the required weight also proved very difficult. People parking their cars up must have thought I was nuts. I mean… who turns up for a walk in the mountains with a pack of dumbbells and the bathroom scales?

Eventually I was happy with the reading on the scales and the weight. Well, not actually happy with the weight I was going to be carrying on my back but you know what I mean. I usually try and take a photo or video of the scales showing the weight but it was very difficult to do this in this scenario as I couldn't pick the weight up with one hand and have the camera in the other hand and hold it on the scales in such a way to see the digital reading. To save any further frustration I just decided that my subscribers would have to trust me, and hurled the 200lb pack onto my back and proceeded towards the mountain path.

For the first few metres the thought popped into my head… "this isn't too bad actually." However, I can well and truly say that I underestimated this challenge. I even remember speaking to my friend Clive in the gym the previous day and I was saying this was going to be the easiest one for me. He disagreed of course, but me a young whipper snapper at the time thought otherwise.

My plod up the mountain path became slow, with many a hiker passing me, giving confused and concerned looks as my heavy breathing turned into more of a pant, the swear words came out of my mouth and I began to pull some comical faces.

Several people actually stopped and asked if I was OK and I had to explain that I was doing a charity challenge, I'd already run 10 miles this morning and that I had a back pack full of dumbbells.

It very quickly became apparent that putting the rucksack down to rest and picking it up was very challenging and potentially dangerous. Not only to save ripping the strap off the pack but also trying to get up was a feat in itself. I'd have to almost lie on the floor, attach the pack to me do some kind of sit up into a press up and then stand up. Great care had to be taken, as twisting movements with an uncontrolled load can cause a lot of stress on the spine.

This was my first time walking up Pen-Y-Fan. I really wish I had done some kind of reconnaissance prior as I would have known what to expect mentally. The saying "time spent on reconnaissance is seldom wasted" was more pertinent to me at this point than ever. As I was going so slow, the path seemed to be going on forever. Almost as if I wasn't moving. I had to fight the seeds of doubt that were trying to take root in my mind.

The higher up I got the more rest stops I began to require and this was where I began to seriously regret ditching my warm kit. As my moving time was arduous and my body began producing a lot of sweat, but when I needed to rest, I was spending increasing periods of time not moving, my sweat worked against me and I began getting very cold. The sweat turned into a shiver.

Another mistake became apparent and that was I had massively underprepared my nutrition. I was eating considerably less than what I would normally eat in a day while burning significantly more calories and

 working for longer than what I was used to. But it was too late to try and change things.

Thinking "why didn't I do this or that" really was not going to help me. I was near the top of a cold mountain with a rucksack full of dumbbells, with no kit that could contribute to my survival. I had two choices – abort or proceed. I opted for the latter knowing that I would have to do it quickly. I pressed on, eventually reaching the top of Pen-Y-Fan after about 3 hours. Dragging my pack up to the trig point to prove I had brought it up there I took a photo.

While earlier the mountain was bustling with walkers, I was now all alone at the summit to take my photo and sort myself out. As I was about to set off for the descent, a lone man approached me. Upon seeing me struggling to shift my rucksack off the rocky trig point, he announced "you're either incredibly weak or that's a very heavy pack!"

The grey clag descended upon the summit and there were no more beautiful views to be seen just the bleak grey cloud and no one here other than a complete stranger who didn't know what I was doing to share this physical effort with.

Strapping the rucksack to my back I began the slow descent along the path not realising that going down was actually going to be as hard as going up, if not harder. My legs and knees were sore and felt so weak. I staggered down the path. I was wearing a cheap pair of 8-year-old boots that were in dire need of replacing.

What made this descent worse for me was after about half way down I could literally see my car as I stumbled down the mountain path that seemed a lot rockier than earlier. Yet it never seemed to get any closer.

There was an overwhelming temptation to take the dumbbells out of my pack and ferry them down individually, or just ditch them in a bush and forget about them forever! No one was up here with me; nobody would have known. But no, that would have been cheating. That would have meant failure. Failure is not an option.

As I reached the final stage of my descent with the car park just a few metres away, I was almost delirious. A group of people were hanging around just past the gate at the bottom, near the entrance to the carpark and I became convinced that they were friends of mine who had come to greet me with a warm coffee and some food. From a distance that guy actually looked like my mate Clive! "What was he doing here?" I thought.

Whether there were actually people there or just some kind of mirage to this day I do not know. There were no friendly faces. There was no coffee or hot food.

I crossed the bridge and walked up the small final incline that approached the car park and placed my rucksack on an old crumbling wall to the left of the gate. Pausing and releasing the tension from the straps I actually think I passed out for a few seconds due to the shock. There was approximately 200m left to walk to the car and I was struggling to muster the energy to get there. My mind was looking for easier options – "ditch the pack, walk to the car, drive the car here"

Cue another self-kick up the ass. I am not doing this to take the easy option. In these situations where you feel tired, weak, drained exhausted – the only valid option is to take charge of yourself and finish what you started. I strapped my pack up, walked the last 200m, unloaded the weight into the boot and breathed a sigh of relief. Challenge two out of three complete.

It was now around 1700hrs and all that was left was an hour's drive home and 1,000 pull ups.

At this point, I was very hungry. I'd had two fairly small meals. The next step now was driving down the A470 towards Cardiff. It had always been my intention to stop at McDonalds and refuel with a truck load of carbs, sugar and salt. A large, warm Big Mac Meal with a sweet strawberry milkshake was what I needed.

That would sort me right out.

What actually happened was far from my intended plan. The queue at the Merthyr McDonalds was ridiculous. Aside from my time living in London I have never seen a McDonalds so packed full of people. Except while the service in London is usually very efficient and the customers are usually in a rush – here were families on a day out taking their time and screaming brats asking to be tripped on.

I wasn't in the mood for this. I figured I could drive to Cardiff and get served quicker at a restaurant there! Plus, time was ticking away.

1 hour, later I arrived in Cardiff Bay. Another change of plan. I didn't have time for a big mac, I'd just head in start busting the reps out and eat a bowl of rice while I was doing it.

The plan was to perform 2-5 reps every minute until I had completed 1,000 pull ups. I began this with enthusiasm, with each rep completed I would mark it on a white board. The first couple of hundred were completed fairly quickly. I felt strong and I was trying to film as much of this as I could, with the plan to do some kind of time lapse.

This was quite boring and monotonous. Do some reps, set the timer to rest, do some more reps and repeat. This process went on for a few hours and as I approached the 700's it was early in the morning and I was knackered. I projected that I would likely finish around 0600hrs at my current pace. But as this was being undertaken on my 2 days off – with 7 days straight of work before my next day off I had inadvertently stitched myself up. I had a load of things to do the next day, appointments, some computer work, meal prep and general life admin.

I made a tactical decision to get a few hours sleep, and then resume in the morning with the pull ups and bust out as many as I could throughout the day around my commitments. With that, I had a quick shower and jumped into my bed for a nap.

Sleeping like a baby for about four hours, I woke up so sore you would not believe. Literally everything was sore and bloody hell I was tired! I crawled out of bed, walked straight to the pull up bar and did my first set of pull ups stark bollock naked. (I had scrapped the time lapse idea by this point you will be pleased to hear!)

This was the most volume pull ups I have ever done, and at a hefty bodyweight of 100kg took its toll particularly on my tendons. Toward the end I started to get pins and needles in my hands and forearms, but eventually with some perseverance the final tally was added to the white board as the last rep was completed. With great satisfaction and relief, I wrote "1000" on the board and sat myself down.

That week, I had actually just started a new job as a Fitness Supervisor in a gym. As I started week two in the new job, I could barely move a muscle due to being so sore after this challenge and I was trying to instruct people at fitness!

Lessons

More preparation is required before attempting such tough challenges. I had forgotten my military training from many years prior and overestimated by abilities, making this challenge a lot harder than it needed to be.

My lack of preparedness had forced me to tackle this challenge solely through stubbornness and determination. While I do regret my lack of prep and reconnaissance, I am certainly grateful for this as it served to re-toughen me up and also gave me some harsh lessons to learn.

If I did this challenge again, I would ensure more training, preparation and also more adequate equipment.

In the military they taught us the **7 P's:**

Prior **P**reparation and **P**lanning **P**revents **P**iss **P**oor **P**erformance

How I wish I had not forgotten that lesson. Sometimes however, we have to learn the hard way.

While I enjoyed virtually nothing about this challenge £330 was raised for SSAFA, the Armed Forces Charity.

Focus

"The successful warrior is the average man, with laser-like focus"

-Bruce Lee

FOCUS

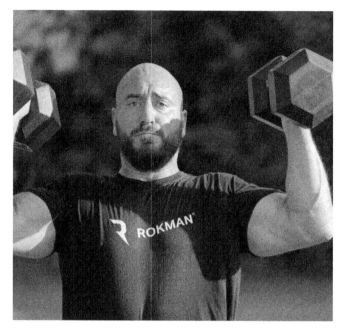

I have a belief that we can achieve anything we set our mind to. The limit is how much focus we are willing to direct towards that specific thing.

By concentrating the effort of the mind and body towards our goals and sacrificing other aspects of our lives that do not correspond to our aspirations we can achieve success.

The Car Pull
Marathon

Car Pull Marathon

I was inspired to undertake this challenge after my friend Jules was given a new lease of life by the miracle workers at the Harefield Hospital in London. Following a genetic lung condition, she gradually over a number of years lost function of her lungs, making life and daily tasks absolutely brutal for her. She needed an oxygen tank to be strapped to her back just to allow her lungs to deliver oxygen to her muscles to enable her to move.

She waited desperately for a transplant and eventually in the early hours of the morning she received a call that suitable lungs were available from a donor. By 0900hrs she was on the operating table.

I met with Jules shortly after her operation and I could not believe the change. I had grown used to seeing my good friend looking pale, ill and tired although that beautiful smile never left her face. I saw the transformation immediately and could not believe how healthy she looked. We had lunch and she explained everything that had happened over the last few weeks. She inspired me to raise money for the Royal Brompton and Harefield Hospital charity so that they can continue to support Jules and provide vital care to those needing new organs.

I decided I was going to pull a car for 26.2 miles. I had heard of someone doing something similar previously and I wanted to try it. I was later informed that it was a chap called Ross Edgley – a gentleman who after conducting diligent research I discovered seems to enjoy extreme challenges even more than I do.

The process of turning an idea into reality began with making enquiries at what I would deem to be suitable locations. However, finding somewhere that would let me do this proved to be quite a challenge in itself.

I'd pretty much decided to forget the idea altogether when an email from Bruntingthorpe Proving Ground slid into my inbox and gave me the green light. They advised me it would have to be a weekend and I could have their track for 24 hours; 1300 Saturday – 1300 Sunday. I checked my rota in work and I had a weekend off.... in just over 2 weeks time. Without hesitation, I booked the track.

This did not give me much time to do a complete switch from bodybuilding training to some kind of strength / endurance hybrid pulling affair... but I will always remember during my final days in Commando training back in 2005 a Royal Marines Adjutant whilst delivering a speech to the Kings Squad stated "do not buckle under pressure, revel in it!" And those words were in my mind and as pertinent to me then as they were during my Kings Squad Week.

For stuff like this, (the way I see it anyway) you will never truly be as ready as you want to be. Sometimes you just have to step out of your comfort zone and roll with it. I actually prefer it like that too, jumping right in the deep end means you quickly have to figure out how to swim.

The track was booked and I went on Amazon and bought the cheapest harness that I could find that looked fit for purpose. Thanks, Jeff Bezos, for making this so easy for me. The idea of spending a load of money for me to raise money sounded pointless. The ultimate aim was to raise money for charity, whereas if I was spending a fortune to do this, I may as well have just donated the money.

I wanted to complete the marathon towing my car, a BMW 525d that weighs in at 1.7 tonnes (my bodyweight at the time was 97kg). Despite numerous people offering to lend me smaller cars or advising me to hire something small like a Toyota Aygo I was determined that I wanted to perform the feat with my car. I knew it would be hard but that is what I wanted. I kept this to myself to avoid the negative advice surrounding my choice and informed my team at the very last minute of my decision.

The Training

What a lot of people don't realise is that I did less than two weeks training for this challenge. I have spoken to numerous people who expected that I would have taken three to six months of preparation to get me ready for it.

This is where the challenge and appeal lay for me. To undertake this massive feat with virtually no prep was right up my alley. While admittedly, I had done a lot of weight lifting over the years so I had a good base of strength. However, doing bodybuilding style workouts does not necessarily translate to the functional pulling on a vehicle and certainly does not lend its way much to endurance. I could count on both hands the number of cardio sessions I had performed in the nine years prior to this point. To put things more into perspective I had worked in a very sedentary job for the previous four years, spending periods of ten to fourteen hours sitting down a day. Bluntly speaking, while I had fairly big muscles, I was not very fit.

The alarm sounded, waking me from my slumber at 0430 on the Sunday morning. Training was about to begin and now there was no backing down. It went from 0 - 100 very quickly! It was early on Sunday morning with 13 days to go and I picked my buddy Chris up and we drove to a local car park for me to tow the car for the very first time! Exciting!! This was a trial run of less than 1 mile for me to see what it felt like, how I could programme my training; what sort of pace I could expect and also for Chris to get used to steering, as he would be there to help on the day of the event.

It was a tough session with many failings and I went away with a sore back very nearly doubting whether I could do the full 26.2 miles. But I went home and had an ice bath and thought it through. Towing the car felt very different to how I had expected, there were a lot of things to consider and it was a lot more technical than just tying a rope to myself, attaching it to the car and running. In the first training session I managed less than 1 mile and I was well and truly knackered. Speed bumps felt like walls, slight inclines felt like mountains and bends in the road wreaked havoc on my spine.

I now knew that nothing I could do in the gym would replicate or prepare me for this challenge. I had hoped a combination of sled pulls / pushes and farmers walks would be suitable for the bulk of my training but that first session made me realise that in order for me to train for this I would have to spend some serious time towing that car.

Knowing that I could not ask Chris to help me train nearly every day for two weeks and then come away with me to the actual event, I turned to the power of social media.

I placed a post on my Facebook announcing what I was going to be doing (with a choreographed video of me falling flat on my face trying to tow the car) and asked if anyone would be able to spare an hour to help me train. I would pick them up, drive to a suitable location and all they had to do was steer the car.

I was astonished by the amount of people who responded offering their assistance, for which I am very grateful. I asked them all what times / dates they were available and as I was working full time too, I'd see if their times fitted in with my schedule. Soon I had compiled a full rota that would see me up until the day before the event.

Some days we were up at the crack of dawn to pull the car around deserted car parks, there were lunch time towing sessions in the blazing hot sun. Leaving work, I'd reply, "Off to the tow the car for an hour," if any of my colleagues asked what I had planned for the evening.

Knowing full well that I didn't have much time to increase my fitness by a dramatic amount, I had to make every training session count. I made sure I covered the following:

- Incline training and hill starts;

- Wet floor - "If it ain't raining, it ain't training" also incline towing in the rain (reduced traction);

- Interval training in small spaces and steady pace on longer roads;

- Weighted training – towing the car with additional weight. This is one of my favourite training methods. I call it accelerated training – I get used to pulling the heavier load and then when it comes to the day of the event pulling the now lighter load feels a lot easier. The psychological benefits of this should not be overlooked.

The training was pretty thorough and I toyed about with different types of footwear that I had available to me to determine what worked best. It turned out that an old pair of Converse All Stars that I had been planning to throw out for some time worked the best. The trouble was they began falling apart, I actually had to super glue the sole together the night before the event.

If it's not obvious to you, the reader, I just want to put this out there. Inclines make a massive difference when towing a car. It is quite easy to pull a car on a flat, level surface and certainly easy whilst on a slight decline! Except in pitch dark when the driver could run you over if you stop! Even 1 or 2% gradient can make a huge difference to the difficulty level.

I also observed that the type of car can make a difference too, some cars are just more streamlined and roll better, and even the height of the towing eye can make a difference to how your power translates to the actual pull on the vehicle. During one training session I switched to use my friends Ford Kuga, which looked like a bigger car than my old BMW, but it was certainly a lot easier to pull.

I'd like to thank the following for their assistance in helping me train:

- Alan King

- Chris Mcjennett

- Chris Probert

- Mark Camilleri

- Mark Cole

- Paul Webber

What I loved about having help from these guys is they are all from different backgrounds and they all offered me their unique view on and gave me advice based on their experiences, which really helped me put things together. They all really got on board and I am eternally grateful for their support and giving up their time to help me train.

One of the best things about training for this challenge was that we were using public car parks, and a man pulling a car around was not something that many people expect to see. This helped with the fundraising efforts and some people wrote out donation cheques there and then, others posted photos and videos of me training to their social media pages.

My final training session was with Mark Camilleri and we had an incredibly productive two hours going up and down an incline in an industrial park. He gave me a good talking to and lot of honest feedback which I really appreciated.

As I spoke to him and realised how much he and the other guys had given up for the cause I was more determined than ever to accomplish this. Aside from my initial mental set back after the first training there was no doubt in my mind that I would be able achieve the full 26.2 miles and every training session gave me more and more confidence. I'd talk about "percentages" when discussing my game plan with anyone who asked. They probably didn't have a clue what I was talking about, but every time something went in my favour, I'd visualise adding a few extra percentages to my advantage.

As I became more and more proficient at pulling the car, I was in a position where I was able to analyse the road ahead for slight bumps and inclines and learned how to apply additional force at the right moments to prevent the car from pulling or slowing down behind me. It was a game of seeing what was ahead, crossing over the bump in the road and then pulling that little bit harder, for that little bit longer, ensuring all four wheels of the car made it over without losing my momentum.

Thirteen days of intense training was complete and as the sun set over Cardiff Bay, Mark wished me luck. I then headed over to Five Guys to fuel up with a big, fat, juicy burger and an insane amount of chips. Devouring that in seconds few, I drove home to begin the laborious task of prepping my meals for the event the next day.

Each meal was prepared into a Tupperware container that I was to eat at specific times during the event. Each tub contained a banana, some malt loaf with butter, and a small pastie. I also had as a treat, a fruity cake that my Mum had baked for me. I knew it was going to be hot and so I also packed a significant amount of bottled water and isotonic drinks in preparation for a long day of sweating. I knew I was going to be isolated on the track, locked in for 24 hours or until the event was completed. So, the working strategy was that the car could store my water and nutrition enabling me to take a break and rehydrate when I needed.

I thought out eventualities to give me the best chance of success. What would happen if the harness snapped? I'd have a rope as a backup. What if my trainers fell apart? I packed a spare set. I had meticulously planned everything to the last detail leaving no stone unturned in my preparation for success. I had a plan, and in my head had assessments and contingencies. I'd even had a contingency plan for if my car got stolen overnight!!

The Event

We set off from Cardiff around 0800 on the morning of Saturday 3rd August 2019. I shared the car with two of my best friends; my old high school buddy Chris Mcjennett and my partner in crime Stephen Foster (an incredibly respected Personal Trainer and legendary motivator). This is the first time that the two of them had met and after a quick introduction we set off on our journey, with my big brother Luke and his girlfriend Sam driving a separate vehicle in convoy to the rear.

The journey from Cardiff to Bruntingthorpe was filled with mixed emotions and high tension. What began with pleasantries soon descended to insults as voices were raised and a heated argument erupted over who is the hottest member of Little Mix. As we approached the services for the sake of any passing members of the public we agreed to disagree. (But everyone knows that it's Jesy).

I parked the car up, turned off the engine and it was at this point as we were stretching our legs that the local media had published an article of what I was planning to do. This prompted my phone to begin detonating with notifications of donations and messages from well-wishers. Reality check! There is no backing down now. This was actually happening.

We arrived in the Leicester area with good time and met up at a local pub with my other best friend Alan King. He had already conducted a recce of the track and spotted a good place for us to meet and have a drink with some snacks. We were feeling pretty peckish at this point and the pub put on some chicken sandwiches to top up our energy levels.

The time quickly approached 1300 and we made our way to Bruntingthorpe Proving Ground where we met with the security guard who gave me a VHF Radio for communication with them and read me the riot act as he lay down the rules.

After a slow trawl around the track in the cars to get to our starting point, I got changed into my shortest short shorts and limbered up.

Under my direction, the guys got to work preparing the vehicle for the challenge and filling it up with water and the snacks I had prepared the night before into little containers to provide me with the right nutrition at the right times.

And there we were. As the sun bore down on Bruntingthorpe Proving Ground, I stood facing the slight incline that led 1 mile or so into the distance. The surreal, desolate nature of the location, with old airplanes strewn between the tracks, like some aviation graveyard added to the bizarre task that I was about to undertake.

I leaned into my harness. The hand brake was removed. With the countdown of "3,2,1 GO!" ensued the slowest start of any vehicle on that track ever.

Breaking It Down

The circuit was approximately 2 miles long, this I told myself meant that I had to do 1 lap - 13 (and a bit) times to reach my goal of 26.2 miles. This is called the chunking method and it is commonly used to break down large tasks into small manageable chunks. I did two weeks of training for this event, with most sessions totalling approximately 1-2 miles of distance.

People would say to me in those weeks, "How are you going to pull it for 26.2 miles if you have only done such short distances?" I would reply with a smile, that I know I can pull it for 1 mile, so all I have to do is do that 26 times.

A couple of people actually told me that I was not going to be able to complete it, that it was impossible to do a marathon whilst pulling a 1.7 tonne 5 Series BMW. I don't blame them for doubting me, but here's a life lesson. Tell a former Royal Marine that something he wants to do is impossible and he will go out of his way to prove you wrong.

It quickly became time to put my money where my mouth is. While I didn't have enough time during training to make huge improvements to my endurance, I spent most of the sessions focussing on techniques and tactics. I observed that athletes who pull vehicles have a tendency to lean forward with their shoulders into the harness. I found that it was more comfortable for me to load my glutes and push into the harness and focus on hip drive for the vast majority of the distance. (I did employ the former method in certain circumstances, such as on hill starts). Luckily, I am blessed with pretty solid glutes.

The first lap was pretty enjoyable, my support team walked it with me. I was sweating buckets due to the sunshine and heat, so I made sure I was staying hydrated and checking my urine regularly to keep it clear, although it took me some hours to achieve this! This is one of the things they taught us in the Marines – to check if you were adequately hydrated. To this day however, I don't think my non-military friends who were present with me fully understood what I was talking about when I kept running into the bushes, returning to announce whether I was "pissing clear" or not…. But they were watching me attempt to do a marathon towing my car without question, so I can only guess that they are used to my antics by now.

The first few laps served as a way of learning the track, I broke the track down in my mind and established that it was comprised of four different sections:

Section 1 – the long incline bit (Just under 1 mile)

Section 2 – the hard bendy incline bit

Section 3 – the easy bit (mainly flat but combined with a decline)

Section 4 – the hardest bit (an incline that led to and continued into a bend)

There was also a chicane that on some laps had to be negotiated, I'd use this chicane as a change of scenery sometimes.

As I went into the event, I expected my first few laps to be the quickest and then slow down and struggle after the 4-mile point. However, to our surprise the complete opposite happened! The first lap was actually one of the slowest, and every lap then until about the half way point became quicker and quicker.

Unknown to me, Alan kept social media updated and checked the donation amount and eventually he called out that we had hit the £1000 mark which was the target. Mission not quite accomplished, I had to finish what I had started. Spirits were high and I don't know about the rest of the team, but this certainly made me feel better.

As the sun began to subside and the air became cooler, I was able to catch up with my hydration. I wasn't sweating as much which was very welcome. As I pulled against the harness, I tried to make every step as powerful and efficient as possible, making sure my legs were doing the work, but I was keeping my body tight and pushing into the harness with my hands; total body tension.

The night began to creep in and concerns were raised among the team that we would lose visibility. I remained convinced that our eyes would adjust and not to worry or use torches / headlights as this would ruin our natural night vision. A lot of people don't realise that after about 40 minutes your eyes adjust to the dark and you can actually see quite a bit, especially on a clear night when there is ambient light from the moon, stars and nearby cities. Only thing is, even the slightest exposure to white light can ruin this night vision and then you pretty much have to start from scratch.

One of the tricks I picked up from the Royal Marines was to keep our shooting eye closed when experiencing lit situations so that we can preserve our night vision in that eye. Sixteen years later, I still use this technique to this day, although for slightly less exciting purposes, such as when I get up in the middle of the night to go to the bathroom.

What I didn't consider however, was that the person steering the car would not be able to see! Lights from the dashboard and screen inhibited the driver's vision and it became difficult for the driver to steer the car to stay directly behind me. This caused me a great deal of pain on the long straight as I could feel the car veering off behind me and putting a lot of strain on my back, forcing me to work harder as I now needed to generate more force to move the car forward.

If the car was not directly behind me, at an angle for example that would mean only a small % of my leg drive was actually pulling the car forward as some of my force would dissipate effectively trying to pull the car to the side.

It was this lap that really took it out of me. The long straight felt longer than ever. It felt like I'd never get to the top, checkpoints that we had established felt further apart and I went into an almost trance like state as fireworks from some nearby party erupted overhead.

I switched my brain off to ignore the pain and focussed on a point to the front. My body went to work, on auto pilot. One foot after the other, pushing, driving down keeping the momentum. A steady, monotonous plod constantly overcoming the friction to keep the car wheels moving.

Steve was walking backwards in front of me as a guide, his white t-shirt became my target. I focused on the white blur that was Steve a few metres to my front in the darkness and I told my body to just plod forward. At one point Steve was talking to me and I didn't even acknowledge him as I had sunk so deep into the zone that I had seemingly disengaged from reality. (Sorry Steve). I had to reassure him that I was fine and that this was just my method of getting through it. When undertaking extreme challenges, I have found I am not a great conversationalist.

Sometime around midnight, the rain came in. From where my body had been so hot in the day, the cool water on my skin mixed into my clothes that were already drenched with sweat. Combined with the physical stress I had subjected it to, resulted in the inevitable drop in body temperature. I could feel myself getting colder and colder as my heart began to pump blood away from my extremities.

Other than that, the rain had no effect on my ability to pull the car around the track. I had worried that I would slip or lose traction but whether it was the training, drills or my ancient converse shoes, I was able to continue my slow yet powerful plod around the track.

We would stop for breaks at set scheduled times and regardless of how I was feeling, we agreed to stop at specific distances. I reverted to the "wet and dry" routines from my military days. As soon I stopped, the harness would come off, I'd rip my cold, wet top off and put on a dry one and then refuel, rehydrate, and keep myself moving. At one point however, I was that cold I had to sit in the car and wait for my body to warm up. I should have packed a fleece! Hindsight is such a wonderful thing.

As quickly as it came, the rain stopped. It was at this point that it dawned on me that all the calories I had been ramming into my mouth had to go somewhere.

They'd gone to my stomach and seemed to be wedged in there. I felt like I was heavily constipated, and I became very concerned that due to my exertion it may be ejected out involuntarily.

With that in mind, I disappeared to the on-site cabin where a toilet was located. I grabbed some wet wipes (just in case) and sat on the toilet for about 15 minutes to no avail. I took a deep breath and stumbled back over to the car (was about a 5-minute walk from where the car had been left). The guys were waiting for me and thought I'd done a runner!

At about 5 am, my brother Luke sent a text message saying that he was doing a McDonald's run and as the lads placed their orders the thought of eating a Big Mac made me feel sick (even though I love them!). I asked for a latte – some caffeine and milk would be exactly what I needed and I'd appreciate the warming effect a hot beverage has. This ensued the longest break we had. I think it was about an hour, maybe more. I had lost track of time.

As first light dawned, we discussed various different tactics and techniques to try and make things easier. It became apparent to me that I was pulling most of this marathon up an incline. I'd certainly made this a lot more difficult than it needed to be. I remember at one point my rattle came out of the pram and voicing my frustration to the team that I was only supposed to be doing a marathon and not a marathon up a hill!

Pulling the car up an incline and on tight bends were starting to take their toll on my body and my mind. I started coming up with all sorts of ideas to take this out of the equation. I offered a suggestion that I would pull the car along the straight section, then take the harness off, and one of the guys could turn the car around and then reconnect the harness and then I'd pull it along the straight again. I'd hit a bit of a wall, and my mind was desperately seeking alternative solutions to make things easier.

There were some concerns from Steve about the impact this was having on my body. In particular the sections where I was pulling the car around bends on the incline, with the driver not being able to see me. This therefore made it difficult for him to position the car directly behind me, causing unnecessary torque on my spine.

After announcing my idea of just pulling on the straight section; The consensus from the team was pretty much, "Do what you want," and we had all but agreed to do this idea when my mind went into gear. There's a saying, a mantra almost that I tell myself in such scenarios, "You've hit your wall, get over it."

I had a quiet word with myself, pulled it together – remembering the ice baths, the cold water, remembering who I am and my training. As the team were discussing their new roles within this change of strategy, I began to compose myself. My inner strength rose like a phoenix. This is my favourite part of these sort of challenges. When I am tired, beaten, broken, cold and with so much hard work left to do – something awakens within.

There was an old saying when I was a Royal Marine recruit, that was, "When you think you're at your limit – you're only actually at 40% of your capacity," (or words to that effect). I am not sure where this originated from, but since then I have heard former Navy SEAL David Goggins describe the same thing. What this means is that when you think that you have done enough and you're exhausted and can't go any further your mind and your body can actually do significantly more.

In the early hours of Sunday morning at Bruntingthorpe Proving Ground, I invited my remaining 60% to come out and play.

 There's a lot of discussion around mindset, getting in the zone or bringing your a-Game. Whatever you choose to call it, there certainly is a switch in our brains that we can control **at will** to be able to achieve seemingly impossible levels of physical strength and endurance.

Upon pressing the switch and deploying my physical and mental reinforcements, I turned to the team and much to their confusion, told them that we were going with the original plan. The hard way, that had seemingly broken me only minutes before. "Just two more times," I explained, "and it's done".

Coinciding with my renewed vigour, we were blessed with the most amazing sun rise. It illuminated the runway energising us and like a steam train, I began chugging away up the long incline, my steps becoming more powerful as we went.

As I approached the last mile, my concern shifted to my phone that had remained in the vehicle throughout as the tracker – it was about to run out of battery!

Thinking fast, we had to put the engine on for the car to charge it up, or risk losing the mileage and proof of the distance covered!

Seeing the track in daylight definitely had its advantages. We were able to use of markers on the track - setting targets to get to. I saw it as if I was in the gym doing sets of reps. I'd have to do X number of reps to get the next section where I'd do a few more sets and reps and so on, as the sweat dripped off me on the final bend – the hardest bit was over, the end was in sight.

As the car was steered, propelled by my leg drive to the final section (the long incline) I was determined for a strong finish. Whenever I have run races or half marathons, I have always made a point of sprinting over the finish line – this was my first and only marathon I have ever completed. Even though I was towing a car, this was no different!

Alan called out the distance, informing me that I had just over 1 tenth of a mile left. I really started firing from all cylinders, so much so that Steve (who remained in front of me throughout the entire marathon) and Chris the camera man had to start running to avoid being mowed down by a psyched up ex-Marine pulling a BMW.

My speed increased, my muscles burned, my breathing hastened. I gripped onto the harness, using all my strength to keep driving this car upwards and forwards. My steps became more powerful. Alan shouted out the distance, "26 point 1!" I put everything into the last few strides. As the sweat dripped off me, a small bird flew from the nearby trees just inches away from my face. The end approached, I picked it up, final few steps.

As the shout of "26 POINT 2!!" echoed across the runway, the hand break was applied. I threw down the harness and embraced a very emotional hug off those special people who had helped me through it. I had pulled a 1.7 tonne car for 26.2 miles and Steve Foster became the first person I know to complete a marathon going backwards.

Fun Facts

- I consumed 30 litres of water during this 24-hour period;

- I burned 22,000 calories (according to my tracker);

- I ate that much I blocked the toilet the next day.

One of the best things about this challenge, is that years later, I still receive messages and emails from people saying that they are training for charity challenges similar to this.

What made this challenge really special for me, is that I got to spend an entire 24 hours with some of my best friends and my brother. We're all so busy and this brought us all together and doing what I enjoy the most, I'd probably say that this was one of the best days of my life.

£2,310 raised for the Royal Brompton and Harefield Hospitals Charity, and I hope that this has helped them to continue the work that they do.

The start of the hardest section of the track

Lessons

With some imagination, the necessary focus and a bit of grit and determination we can achieve practically anything. Having never towed a car before, or completed a marathon; to towing an old 5 Series for 26.2 miles with less than 2 weeks of training proves this.

The Mind Has a Toolbox

This is my own personal theory. When you complete some kind of tough task, or challenge; your mind remembers it and more importantly – how you achieved it. That means, when presented with another obstacle in the future you have tools available to overcome it. The more our body and mind have to be pushed, the more tools we have at our disposal.

When I was training for this challenge, it was all I could think about. It seemed like a huge mountain in front of me with no clear cut route and no guarantee of success. But now that I have completed it, it doesn't seem so difficult. I know that I could go back and complete this challenge if I tried it again.

The Chunking Method

I broke 26.2 miles down into tiny 0.25 mile segments and just focussed on completing each one. Nearly anyone can pull a car for 0.25 miles. This method does not apply solely to pulling a car. It can be applied to any huge task.

In this book I speak mainly of physical challenges, but we all have times when we have needed to apply the chunking method to some kind of challenge in our lives.

In 2012, when I was working in security, I was bored as an operator and decided that I wanted to teach security. By 2013, I had qualified as a teacher and started my own training business.

As soon as I got my certificate through, I applied to the awarding body for the qualification that I wished to teach. When they replied, I was absolutely gobsmacked by the amount of work I was going to have to do.

My training company was a one-man band, operating from my bedroom, yet the awarding body demanded the same level of strict criteria as a recognised education establishment, such as a college. I needed a long list of requirements:

- A high standard training facility – that would be inspected to meet strict criteria;

- At least two tutors who could evidence that they had proven experience in teaching and assessing;

- Evidence that my training company had experience of teaching and assessing;

- Independent verifiers from an education background;

- Independent invigilators to-hand for the exam;

- An exam room, separate from the training room that would need to be inspected to meet strict criteria;

- Effective policies on dealing with the learner journey, complaints, disputes, bullying health & safety, privacy, payments, re-tests etc;

- I had to write the training course from scratch, complete with lesson plans to meet the strict criteria of the awarding body.

I had thought that just completing my teaching qualification and having experience within the industry would have been enough, but that was the easy bit!

After being initially disheartened, I looked at each obstacle and racked my brain to figure out how I could deal with each one individually.

I shopped around for a place with a training room I could use and developed a good rapport with a business that I ended up working with regularly.

Concurrently, I contacted an old buddy from the Marines who I knew lived locally and worked away from time to time and was able to work for me while he was home for the course dates. He had experience training Royal Marines recruits so ticked the correct boxes and also had vast experience within the security sector.

A friend of a friend was an experienced school teacher and met the criteria for my independent verifier, so I got her on board to tick a few boxes for me and ensure I was maintaining standards.

I contacted one of my best friends, explained the situation and he was up for being an exam invigilator for the duration of the exam.

As I had only recently qualified, I lacked proven experience in teaching and so did my newly formed training business. This is the bit that proved the most challenging, as to gain this experience I would have to develop a separate course and successfully deliver that.

So that's what I did. I developed a very similar qualification (with a different awarding body). I was able to use what I had put together and the policies and procedures once written up, met the standard for each awarding body.

This took a lot of time, but I worked through it. I had a lot of financial and personal problems at the time as well. I remember for a lot of this I didn't even have a desk to work on. There were some difficult moments, and my friend Alan let me use his house while he was in work. (I think I owe him a large amount of coffee!)

During this time, I was seeing a girl. In her bathroom there was a little ornament. A small stone with the words:

"It always seems impossible, until it is done."

Those words really helped me whenever I saw them and I would use them to strengthen my resolve and help me focus.

Eventually, my hard work paid off. I was awarded the status of an approved training provider by two major awarding bodies to deliver not only one, but four internationally recognised qualifications.

Within a few months, I was delivering training courses not only in the UK but also in Germany and France.

I only operated that business for a couple of years. There had been a rapid increase in requirement for recognised security training within the maritime sector and I had cashed in on this. Whilst the date for mandatory training had passed, there was an awful lot of security companies offering the same security courses and not so many people needing the training.

As I wasn't teaching every day, and after the initial set up was complete, I had a lot of spare time. I had started working in a gym and would eventually step up the rungs of leisure management. I really enjoyed this and worked it around my courses. I would finish at the gym, head to the airport, fly to France deliver a couple of days training on a Superyacht; then head back to work in the gym.

Eventually, working 40-60 hours per week in the gym, I fell behind on the admin side of things for the training business and had Companies House on my case. Rather than spending my time hiding from them, my Company was dissolved. I was actually in Spain at the time starting a YouTube channel when I decided I wasn't interested in working security any more. I had considered branching out to different types of training – Door Supervisor, First Aid etc, but there were a lot of established players in this area and it was not something that I was really that interested in. I was getting a buzz from working in fitness and it seemed to be closely connected to my passion for working out and seeing others achieve their goals.

No Excuses

No Excuses

Writing this book serves as a step out of my personal comfort zone. Whereas I'd much rather be out walking in the woods, enjoying the fresh air, bright green leaves of the trees and listening to the birds singing their jubilant melodies. I'd certainly prefer to be in the gym pumping iron as the weights clang and veins bulge. Instead, here I am slumped over a laptop tapping away furiously at the keyboard.

This sums up what the book is all about. I don't have a writing room, a study or even a desk to write this book on. This book has been written whilst sitting at a battered piano, with noisy builders playing loud music, singing and drilling away for months on end. I have chipped away at it in between clients on a coffee table at the gym, even at times from the seat of my car. As I write this very paragraph, there is a builder on the other side of the window singing a football anthem at the top of his voice.

These things really pissed me off and made writing this book difficult. Difficult to concentrate. And there have been times when I have been so frustrated that I have fallen behind on my timescales and other projects have been affected. But the point is, it would have been all too easy to have used these reasons as an excuse to not complete what I started out.

The exciting thing about self-publishing a book is the opportunity to break some rules! Just like with making YouTube videos I enjoy breaking the rules of traditional media. Having enjoyed Media Studies at school, the new way that the latest generation consumes content is shattering all the traditional moulds of entertainment. I can only imagine that fat cat media bosses are desperately trying to change their content strategy so that they can remain current in the years to come.

While I know absolutely nothing about publishing books, I am very excited to create my own rules, lay down my own path and see what happens.

The Piano Carry

The Piano Carry

For those of you that have not earned the Coveted Green Beret, I would like to take these moments to describe how it feels once you crack 32+ weeks of training at Lympstone and become a Royal Marines Commando. You feel ten feet tall.

Many Royal Marines are so proud of their berets, that even when deployed on ops would rather wear their "Green Lid" over a ballistic helmet any day of the week (the Troop Commander would insist on the latter, however). It was even joked that the Green Beret was bullet proof and aspiring recruits would not dare even touch a Green Beret, for fear of some superstitious curse that would foil their efforts to achieve what they were so desperately trying to earn.

I'd like you to take some time to imagine how you would feel during this moment – after spending the better part of a year sweating, bleeding and shedding tears to finally have this mythical item of head dress presented to you, knowing full well that so many others have failed. At that moment, particularly at such a young age you almost feel like you are the first person to have achieved anything spectacular.

There was a bit of a joke in the Marines when discussing physical challenges (particularly those undertaken by civilians) that if they weren't conducted with kit on, in our eyes… it didn't count! What I am trying to say is Royal Marines are particularly hard to impress.

December 2005 - Having not long completed Royal Marines training I was reading a news article, learning of an old piano being discovered under a pile of rocks near the summit of Ben Nevis – the highest mountain in the United Kingdom. It was unclear at the time how this got there, but it was likely left by a group of removal men who carried it up as a team back in the 80's.

Stories emerged of a Scottish strong man Kenny Campbell who carried a 226lb church organ to the top of the mountain. This was the leading theory at the time and rumour had it he even played "Scotland the Brave" at the summit! It seems Kenny did not leave his church organ at the summit and he is well known to have carried many heavy objects up and down Ben Nevis to raise money for charity.

I remember seeing a picture of a guy, hunched forward with a piano on his back plodding up the gradient. I was impressed, and I could not comprehend the levels of strength and endurance required to be able to perform such a feat. These thoughts stayed in my mind for many, many years.

Christmas Day 2018 – having recently scaled Ben Nevis from the North side and remembering the story of Kenny Campbell and his church organ, I was inspired and as I sat down to enjoy the festivities with my friend Steve… I proclaimed that I was going to carry a piano to the top of a mountain. While this was met with hoots of laughter, I had plenty of intention but no actual plan on what I was going to be doing, where I was going to get a piano from or how I was going to get there.

The human brain is an amazing thing. There are so many processes going on behind the scenes and we cannot even comprehend the true power of what we are capable of. All it takes is a simple idea, that starts off as a seed and slowly begins to develop, nurtured by our subconscious.

How many times have you been in the shower enjoying the warm water and soapy suds when a random epiphany hits your like a freight train? Or been lying in bed and suddenly the solution to some complex problem that has been plaguing you for weeks is inserted into your brain? That's kind of what happened here, and this is one of my favourite things about doing challenges and also about being a YouTuber. Starting off with an idea and watching it develop and grow.

I initially was presented with several hurdles to overcome.

- I needed a piano.

- I needed a mountain – working strategy was initially Pen-Y-Fan in South Wales, however the National Trust insisted on a comprehensive risk assessment and insurance before they could agree to use their land.

- I needed to figure out where I could store the piano when I got one and how I could get it to the mountain on the day and where I could take it afterwards.

- I needed to figure out a way that this could be undertaken without putting any members of the public at risk, and also without causing any damage to the mountain or paths.

- I needed contingencies – what if I got injured half way up?

- How the hell was I going to train for this one?!

Whilst there were many other things I needed to consider before I could even attempt this challenge, dates and locations needed to be agreed. A piano was acquired towards the end of 2019 and I found a place to store it. This coincided with me moving out of my apartment so I timed it perfectly. I remember vividly hiring a van, driving for 8 hours to bring the piano back, returning the van, cleaning my apartment overnight, moving out and then being in work for 0530 in the morning without sleeping and while suffering with the flu. These things always come at the most inopportune of moments.

My training programme began in earnest – mostly gym based with lots of squats, deadlifts, and farmers walks to begin with. This was to build a base level of strength and then I introduced weighted ruck sack walks on a treadmill at 18% incline for 4 miles. These sessions were brutal. I'd increase the weight by 5kg every session. I believe in constantly trying to progress to force the body to adapt. The load quickly became heavy. The running machines, not designed for such heavy loads would struggle to raise to the selected incline, each step would cause the treadmill to bounce up and down slightly. I was sweating buckets and getting some funny looks – although this is something I am very used to! The sessions were fuelled by water, bananas and home-made isotonic drinks.

I built the training up, then focussed on unilateral work and stepping movements. I made sure that all weights lifted were 150-200kg so my body could get used to handling the weight of the piano. Gym equipment is not built to handle this type of training. I had to find work arounds to make sure I wasn't breaking the kit in the gym, such as placing blocks underneath the steps to add extra support so it wouldn't buckle under the weight of me and what I was lifting.

By the start of 2020 I was hiking up and down Pen-Y-Fan regularly, often with a weight in my rucksack. My plan was to familiarise myself with the route. Learn it like the back of my hand. I wanted to know the exact % of each incline, which parts were going to be hardest, and which bits would be easiest. I needed to consider any rest break areas for myself and also for any of my friends who wanted to come along with me. Concurrently I was liaising with the National Trust and having some hilarious conversations with insurance brokers.

The reason I chose Pen-Y-Fan was because it is nice and close to home in Cardiff, and it meant I could do the trip in one day without having to take additional time off work, or incur overnight expenses. I was raising money for charity and as before I figured that if I am going to be spending more doing the challenge than was actually donated, then I'd may as well just donate that money to charity rather than go on a jolly.

My strength wasn't increasing as quickly as I had hoped. But I proceeded forwards through the different stages of training and eventually moved onto stage 3 – which involved carrying the piano on my back. I figured out that the best way to do this, was to get a couple of cam straps, loop them around the piano and just pull them tight around my shoulders and then do a bit of a squat to take the weight of the piano. The first time trying this was quite a daunting experience, a leap of faith, but I quickly became a pro.

By February 2020 Stage 3 was beginning to progress. I'd mastered the knack of getting the piano onto my back and now I needed to learn to travel with it. This involved me walking on flat ground around the streets of Cardiff. Seeing the shocked expressions on the faces of people I passed was very humorous indeed. One of my concerns was the effect of wind on the piano. Knowing that it was a large object, my surface area had increased massively. I was lucky that in Wales it is always pretty windy, so I soon experienced this first hand. My stabilisers and core strength would have to pretty robust to be able to maintain structural integrity under such an awkward heavy load, combined with unpredictable wind resistance.

The first time I carried the piano

But alas, all this training was in vain. Covid-19 began spreading around the UK and I decided that I was going to postpone the training and the challenge. Gyms were closing, the country went into lockdown and I was halfway between moving home again, half of my belongings were in storage, some in the car boot and some at my mums.

While I was very fortunate to have a rack of dumbbells, I gave some out to friends and kept a few with me. Without the gym a lot of people struggled to maintain muscle and strength during lockdown, I was unable to train at home due to space. I bought an infantry bergen (a military rucksack) and loaded it up with two dumbbells, water, resistance bands, roll matt, first aid kid and sunglasses. I would walk for a few miles until I found a suitable place to train and would begin circuit training in a field or car park.

As the weeks went by, I began to realise that my body was getting stronger at carrying weight. I was gradually increasing the amount of weight I was taking with me to work out, and this resulted in my legs becoming stronger and having more endurance. I loved my lockdown circuits. Legs were trained with loaded carries before and after, with weighted burpees and sprints during the workout. My upper body was trained with press ups, bent over rows, dumbbell clean and press from the floor, mountain climbers and planks. I started doing hill training and my workouts actually began to revolve around carrying the weight, rather than the loaded carry being my travel to working out. The weight in the pack got heavier and heavier until eventually I was walking up hills carrying 130kg in my bergen! I remembered my roots. I am a former Royal Marines Commando, carrying heavy objects on my back over extended periods of distance is in my DNA.

One challenge of all the outdoor training was avoiding members of the public and their out-of-control dogs. They didn't understand that I was carrying a huge amount of weight on my back and by trying to keep my distance from them so as not to kill them if the strap snapped and landed on their child or dog. But needless to say, the public very rarely tried to keep any form of distance from me and on one occasion I had to change direction suddenly to avoid a dog that the owner allowed to come charging towards me and my Achilles tendon popped in a spectacular manner! While this was only a mild set back in the grand scheme of things, it would come back with a vengeance later on.

Summer was cracking on and lockdown was eased. It became apparent to me that I was at the strongest I had been for a while. I thought to myself when would I ever get the opportunity to train like this again? I was now custom built for carrying heavy objects on my back and better yet – carrying them up hills. I looked at the UK Covid rates, I was back working full time and doing my self-employed work on the side so wasn't getting as much chance to train as I had done previously. The weather would be getting colder, darker and wetter soon and I could see the Covid rates increasing during the Autumn / Winter which would undoubtedly lead to tighter restrictions.

I had a narrow window of opportunity to undertake this challenge. I scrapped the idea of Pen-Y-Fan and went with the closest mountain to home – Garth. At 307m in elevation it is quite possibly the smallest mountain in the UK. However, the distance from my starting point was 2 miles, which was a similar distance I would have ascended at Pen-Y-Fan. It's just the starting point would have been higher.

Garth has an interesting story behind it. Local legend states that when the English were surveying mountains in the area, they determined that Garth was a hill rather than a mountain. British Ordnance Survey defined a mountain as anything above 1000ft (304 metres). The locals, in a bid to make the English look foolish built up a mound on the top of the hill, so that when the English returned to conclude their surveys the hill was now classified as above 1000ft and therefore a mountain.

How true this story is, I don't know. What makes Garth Mountain even more interesting is if you go off the beaten track you will find old mine shafts that lead inside the mountain into old networks of caves and quarries and an underground lake with mysteriously blue water.

Garth has amazing views over Cardiff and the surrounding area. This had an added advantage for me. As it meant that driving to work each morning, I'd be able to look up and see it.

Defeated Before It Began

I chose Sunday 13th September 2020 to make the piano
attempt. My girlfriend Nez and I had performed recon
of the route twice and I had walked the entire route in
my head with the piano on my back. Nez was a huge
help for me during this challenge, helping me train for
it, accompanying me on many walks and always
keeping us smiling. But as time got closer to the
proposed date, things were to begin working against
me. The 7 day working weeks, the daily 3am alarm
clocks, the longs hours in work and the hard training
began to take their toll on me. I was struck down with
a very nasty cold about ten days before the event was
due to start. I had to self-isolate, taking time off work
and get tested for Covid (which fortunately was a
negative result) however I felt very weak. Terry

Rosoman from Rokman helped out massively, putting together a press release and very quickly my inbox began to fill with emails and my phone lit up like a Christmas tree with calls from local journalists.

I really felt the pressure with this one. Because my car pull marathon had attracted international attention, there seemed to be a great deal of expectation from me. Whereas with the car pull marathon, people were saying that there was no way I'd be able to do it, and I just slipped under the radar, went out and not only completed it, but I captured it on camera in beautiful 4K. This time there were headlines telling the world that a former Royal Marine and strong man is going to carry a piano up a mountain and making out like I was some kind of Superhero.

As the week ticked by, I was willing my immune system to fight off this cold, flu or whatever it was. I had an intense programme lined up that was engineered perfectly and designed specifically to culminate with the Garth piano carry, but I had to scrap this for fear the physical stress would make my ill body even weaker. On top of this, my Achilles tendon pain from the Summer flared up and made walking particularly uncomfortable. All of this meant that my confidence was at an all-time low, I'd been training for this for so long. An internal battle raged within my mind, arguing with myself - I was ready over a month ago and I should have done it then. My current condition feeling nowhere near the level I was at towards the end of July. I did not even want to tell any more people that I was going to be doing this for fear of having to call it off or that I'd fail and humiliate myself. Donations were coming in and I was feeling like a fraud.

As the day of the event dawned, I still felt like utter garbage. While everyone around me believed in me, self-doubt had firmly planted its roots inside. Normally in these situations we can rely on our training, but my training had gone backwards in the last few weeks and I had missed out on the intense programme I had planned. I had let myself down. I instantly became my number one enemy and my biggest threat to success.

The Event

At around 0500 on Sunday 13th September, I had a very quiet word with myself in the bathroom. I reminded myself of all the training I had done that year. I told myself that there is no one on this world more prepared than I was right now in that moment to carry a piano to the top of the mountain and bring it back down. I remembered that once you get through the self-doubt and darkness there is always light. I thought of the cold water, the ice baths and the personal mantra that would play in my head during those sessions.

I began to hear the voice of David Goggins in my head, telling me that I was, "Going to die without even trying to reach my full potential."

Looking at myself in the mirror, I told myself, "You've walked this in your head, you have already been to the top of this mountain. You said you were going to do it – so you're going to do it". And with that I emerged from the bathroom without a doubt in my mind that I would pull this off.

Those few moments I spent talking to myself were without a doubt the deciding factor in how this challenge played out. Yes, I performed a good twenty minutes of muscle activation afterwards, but by engaging the mind I was fired up. Tying the laces of my boots in a double knot, I was determined to not only carry the piano up the mountain.... I wanted to run up there with it!

Fortunately, I had been quite organised in setting this challenge up. The piano was loaded and good to go from the night before. This meant that in the morning all I'd have to do is get up, have a big breakfast and get myself to the town of Gwaelod-Y-Garth (Welsh for

"Foot of Garth") and get started. I had opted for an early start, as the starting point was just off the main road and I didn't want to fall in the bad books of the local Constabulary by causing an obstruction on the highway trying to get a piano on my back!

Terry arrived nice and early and as usual was full of energy and ready to get started. I posted a live video announcing that I was about to start the challenge.

It was a beautiful summer morning; the only noise was the birds singing in the luscious green trees. The air felt fresh on my lungs, and I could tell it was going to be a scorcher later. My goal was to get this piano on my back and power up that incline. I can honestly say that I trained incredibly hard for this. I was so prepared mentally and physically (aside from my earlier set back) that once we started moving it became like clock-work. I had a few friends with me; Chris, Mark, Jules, Terry and my girlfriend Nez in a support van who was always nearby in case I snapped my knee and we needed to get the piano loaded up quickly and me rushed off to hospital.

We started off near the bottom by the pub, tackling the notorious hair pin bend on what is arguably the steepest bit. As the support struggled to negotiate the incline and bend, I plodded up the mountain road behind it. This had a massive psychological advantage for me. I'd get the steep bit out of the way while I was fresh, and knowing that I could complete this would mean I could complete any other gradient on the walk. I just had to get to the top of this slope first!

I don't know if you have ever tried moving a piano, not only are they exceptionally heavy (nearly 400lbs!) but they are a very awkward shape of wood and iron. The sheer size of them makes them difficult to move even between rooms of a house let alone carry them 2 miles up 30% gradient and uneven terrain! I am often asked how did I do that? It was a simply process. I trained and prepared for it. So even though actually carrying an awkward wooden object that was nearly twice as much as my bodyweight was heavy and my muscles in the quads and glutes were screaming and even trembling at certain points, I knew that I just had to focus on each individual step. One foot in front of the other. I knew I could do 10 steps. So, if I kept going and do another 10 steps, and then another 10 steps, next thing you know it's 100 steps and before I knew it, I've done a kilometre.

As I ascended the mountain path taking the piano higher and higher the sweat was dripping off me, my breathing deep as I focused on keeping my whole body tight and strong. One wrong move, slip or trip could be devastating for me. If things went South, I could put myself out of action for a very long time, even permanently.

The ironic thing about this challenge is that I did it to raise money for a charity that helps people with lung problems, and I spent the whole thing out of breath – which really put things into perspective. My friend Jules, who had a double lung transplant in 2019 at the Harefield Hospital thus inspiring the whole thing even said: "this is what it was like for us all the time." So, it's hard for me to complain really.

It may seem like I am just some guy going out, hauling a piano up a mountain and then heading home… but I can assure you that there needs to be robust planning and contingencies. I have massive respect for the environment and the mountain.

The piano had to be carried to the top and then brought down and done so in a manner that would not damage the ground or cause danger to anyone else. While I accept that I am putting myself at risk of physical injury I do not want my challenges to ever put anyone else at risk. Meticulous planning is imperative.

About half way up we had a quick rest stop and a bit of food. Spaghetti Bolognese – my favourite! It was at this point someone observed that the wooden frame of the piano was digging into my back and had penetrated the skin and was causing me to bleed. This did not bother me too much as I proclaimed that padding was "for wimps." My girlfriend Nez had other thoughts. She was worried that I'd have hideous scars for the rest of my life and insisted I consider padding it out. I had brought a gym mat with me and this provided an ideal layer of padding, which actually did make carrying the piano on my back a lot easier. Now, I only had to focus on the pain in my muscles.

It was at this point that we began encountering members of the public, many were conducting their morning exercise routines and some were doing charity events of their own. I distinctly remember a few cyclists huffing and puffing battling the incline, in a world of hurt of their own, only to come around the bend and see me carrying a piano up the same slope.

This was the first time I had ever really engaged with members of the public while doing one of my challenges and was really helpful in my fund-raising efforts. Everyone who passed stopped and asked what the hell I was doing. This ultimately led to the conversation that I was doing it for charity and many took photos to share on social media.

My technique for this just involved a lot of patience. Short powerful steps, with my whole body braced to support the awkward weight of the mammoth musical instrument on my back. At about three quarters of the way up, I began to feel my quadriceps quivering. I could feel the onset of cramp. I called a quick rest stop, where I could re-hydrate and do some stretches. The last thing I wanted was for my quads to fully cramp up whilst I had the piano on my back. "Sort the cramp out before it becomes a problem," I told myself.

After a short break the cramp was dealt with. I progressed with the journey. As the path began to level off, we were met with another hairpin bend that would take us up another steep section. This was going to be tough, but I embraced the challenge. There seemed to be quite a lot of people around at this point, lots of people out for their morning walk. I was making quite a spectacle of myself huffing and puffing with a piano on my back. But this audience only served to renew my vigour. I was aware that there were people filming me with smart phones, and watching to see what I was doing. I attacked the slope. I wanted a strong performance. This is what I had been training for. Head down, one step at a time. In my mind I knew that this was the pen-ultimate steep bit. I'd have a rest at the top and enjoy the view.

The next section, whilst not being so steep presented its own challenges that needed to be overcome. The terrain was uneven, with small holes and bumps in the ground. What concerned me most however, was the grass was wet and slippery in places. I'd have to be very careful to negotiate the correct route. I was looking ahead at the various different options I could take, stepping slowly and cautiously whilst bracing the piano on my back.

My ankle stability was tested on the uneven ground, but the training paid off as slowly but surely, I neared my destination. This was it, only one hurdle left. The mound.

Approaching the summit, the steep mound appeared in view. Glistening slightly with the morning dew, I'd have to be careful not to slip. A small crowd had gathered at the base of the mound and I knew that I only had one shot at this. I placed the piano down a short distance from the mound. I considered powering straight up; however, I wanted to rest my legs as this would require significantly larger steps than what I had been doing to that point and also, I wanted to check the most appropriate route of approach.

After my short break I strapped the piano to my back, stared up at the summit, took a deep breath, braced myself and took the weight of the piano on my back. Like a medieval knight launching an attack on a fort I stormed towards the mound.

The flat approach offered me some momentum, and I quickly reached the steep uneven terrain of the mound. As my slow trepid steps ascended the mound, cheers erupted from onlookers. I dug deep and launched an all or nothing assault to step up the final section of the mound. This section was fairly steep and required me to lift my tired legs higher and higher, which could have gone either one way or another. Fortunately, it went in my favour and I was able to achieve sufficient traction and deliver enough power from my leg to drive me and the piano up. Then the mound levelled off. As the cheers grew in volume, the intensity of the effort required to move decreased. I'd won the battle. I was at the top. I had done it.

The piano was placed securely on the ground next to the Trig Point at the summit of Garth. Mobile phones and video cameras were in my face as the moment was recorded and live streamed on social media.

There was a jubilant atmosphere at the summit. It was such a surreal setting, with beautiful views over Cardiff, The Brecon Beacons and even as far as Somerset. People took it in turns to play tunes on the piano. The highlight was most certainly the young girl aged around 7 having a go at the piano at the top of a mountain.

Unfortunately for me, video emerged of my pathetic attempts to play "The Gael" from the last of the

Mohicans which typically enough was broadcast over National TV. Believe it or not I had actually spent a bit of time trying to learn to play some tunes, but I am not musically gifted, and in all the excitement my mind went blank. I'll stick to lifting heavy objects and leave making the music to people who actually know what they're doing.

I thoroughly enjoyed this challenge and the piano is occasionally played by my girlfriend Nez. Even Spice the cat has a go from time to time. It also doubles up as table for me to write this story on my laptop.

Fun Facts

- This challenge despite being years in the making, was completed in three hours.

- There was no time to relax after this had finished – we had to take the piano down into the house and then return the hired van.

- Afterwards I celebrated with a cup of coffee in the garden, my first and only McDonalds in a year and then went to visit my mum (where we had even more food!)

- £2,203 raised for the Royal Brompton and Harefield Hospitals Charity.

The Piano resting at the top of Garth Mountain

I want to say a huge thank you to those who supported me and helped me with this challenge.

Lessons

Planning and preparation as always are the most fundamental things to increase the likelihood of success. However, things don't always go according to plan…

In this case, things went wrong from all angles and got in my way; from a pandemic, gyms being closed to an Achilles tendon injury. And on the day of the event my plan was unravelling and my mind began the spiral of defeat. SNAP OUT OF IT! Rely on the training and take charge of the mind at the earliest opportunity. Remember:

Don't buckle under pressure, Revel in it!

We don't have control over everything going on around us. But we can control how we react to dynamic circumstances and by focussing on the things we can control that we can determine our success or failure.

Pain Management

Pain Management

I lay back in the chair and the light shone in my eyes. My mouth was being held open. Nervously, I looked up and a man with a medical mask peered over me.

He brandished a small drill, pushed it into my mouth and with an excited whir it began to bore directly into my teeth. The pain was excruciating. I wanted to scream, but I couldn't. I was afraid that if I moved my mouth the drill would do further damage to my teeth.

Wave after wave of painful vibrations reverberated through my jaw. As the drill kept grinding away at my enamel, seemingly going on forever. All I could do was focus on a point out to the front. I kept my gaze on that. No one else cried or screamed when they went to the dentist, I had to be tough. My mum was there I didn't want her to see me crying or getting upset.

This was a childhood visit to the dentist, I hadn't looked after my teeth as a junior and the dentist had to drill out the fillings that had rotted away.

This was surely a standard procedure? Only that the dentist had forgotten to give me a local anaesthetic. I did not realise this at the time, until I went in a few weeks later to have the other half of my mouth done on the same procedure and I felt no pain whatsoever.

At a young age I learnt that pain can be managed, I expected it to hurt, as everyone always said they would dread the trip to the dentist. I had assumed that this was just a normal pain. In reality the physical pain hurt like nothing I had ever experienced before, but even as I child I was able to manage it because I knew no different. I thought this was the pain that everyone who ever went to the dentist experienced.

While I never want to experience that again; This shows that our mind can manage pain effectively and allow us to push ourselves outside of our comfort zone when we need to. We have the tools within us to push us through arduous situations. As the Royal Marines say; **It's a State of Mind**.

You do not require months of military training to acquire this specific state of mind that they refer to. The fact of the matter is, you already have it.

100KG
Over
100KM

100kg Over 100km

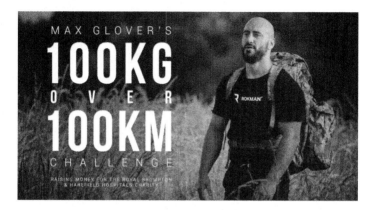

In March 2021 the Royal Brompton and Harefield Hospitals Charity contacted me to ask if I would be interested in taking part in their Heart Vs Lungs 2.0 challenge. This was a bit of friendly competition where two teams of fundraisers compete to see who can raise the most money and also cover the most distance in the month of April. I filmed a warm up video for them to post on their social media channels and I decided that I would also take part to cover distance and raise money to save lives.

I decided to resurrect an old challenge idea that I had envisaged around 18 months prior. 100 miles carrying 100lbs. This however, seemed like quite a light weight for me now, as when I had thought about this challenge, I had not done much in the way of loaded carries. Remembering that I am from the UK and we adopted the Metric System in 1965 and recognising that I seem to enjoy taking strength and mixing it with endurance… why not more than double the weight? – 100kg for 100km! (220lbs) This would be a rucksack full of dumbbells equalling a total of 102% of my bodyweight.

The 100lbs idea was initially supposed to be non-stop however the 100kg challenge was planned to be completed over a number of days. I didn't want to put too much pressure on doing it quickly, after all I wasn't racing anyone and it was part of a challenge that spanned a month, not to mention I had to work, do household chores, prep all my kit / meals and maintain family commitments.

This is what I found hardest about the challenge. For the first time, I wasn't able to just suck it up and plough through to the finish line and then just resume my normal life the next day (albeit a little sore!) This required commitment and organisation.

The Preparation

As usual, I did very little training for this event. It is very likely that I still had a bit of carryover strength left over from the piano carry and training that I had completed seven months earlier. However, I'd also done very little in the way of loaded carries this year and had also ruptured both Achilles tendons exactly two months before this challenge was due to start. In February, I couldn't walk or even move my foot and here I was in April planning to do 100km with a rucksack full of dumbbells on my back.

I'm a bit spontaneous when it comes to these challenges. It was about a week or two beforehand that I'd actually decided I was going to go with this, and so I set up my JustGiving page to try and attract sponsorship to raise money for the hospital's charity Covid-19 fund. The hospital is one of the few cardio respiratory specialists in the UK and had been in the thick of it on the frontline fighting against Covid-19. It was an interesting twist that having cancelled many projects and challenge ideas due to Covid, I was now planning a challenge specifically to support those who were helping patients.

In preparation for this challenge, I came to the conclusion that my infantry bergen that I had purchased less than a year earlier had more or less had its day. While it was still up to the odd trip up the mountains, or a light yomp over a hill, I really did not think it would be up for carrying 100kg for such a long distance. It was time for me to upgrade and I went for the Para field support bergen. Something I had considered a year earlier due to the considerable volume of kit it can carry. The bergen itself looked a hell of a lot stronger and after much deliberation I decided it was the one for me.

When the new bergen arrived, it dwarfed my old infantry pack like the incredible hulk on steroids. I've realised now that I get incredibly excited about new boots and new bergens. This was something I really never cared about in the past or in the military when I didn't have to pay for any of it. Perhaps I am developing some kind of fetish. In a few years time I'll probably be wandering around town in full military attire yelling "GRENADE!" and "FIX BAYONETS!" at the most inappropriate moments.

Putting together a strategy for tough challenges is the best way to tackle them. Yes, our bodies are strong and can adapt but I have learnt from my previous challenges that often a few simple tweaks or a bit of a game plan can make life a lot easier. I had a think of the best way to tackle this challenge and decided that doing too much training could actually be detrimental to my body. Yes, this is not a typo – for this tough challenge I decided I was to do barely any training whatsoever.

I figured that, as the challenge itself will take around 7-10 days to complete, my body would (hopefully) adapt during this time frame. I did a few walks beforehand just to figure out the new bergen, as it was slightly different to what I was used to and also for me to work out pacing and get the feel of carrying 100kg on my back.

If I had six months to prep for this then logically, based on progressive overload, I would have just gradually built the weight up over time. But I had less than two weeks and so I just filled the bergen up with dumbbells until it weighed 100kg, hurled it on to my back and then off I went to do my tests.

These tests were of the kit, but also to see if it was possible for me to do. I knew it was definitely humanly possible to achieve this, however I needed to ascertain what my chances of success were, while considering how long it will take. The risk of aggravating my Achilles tendons was ever present and so I had to think of mitigation measures to decrease the likelihood of doing further damage. Messing up my tendons even further after the injury two months prior was one of the last things I wanted.

Nez and I went away to West Wales to relax for a couple of days before this challenge was due to start. She soon realised that she'd have to pack light as half the boot was taken up with a rather large rucksack full of dumbbells!

4 Dumbbells stacked on top of each other

The Event

Day 1 (Monday)

The first day started off nice and early. My alarm went off at the crack of dawn and as Nez got ready for work, I began cooking an enormous breakfast to fuel me through the day. 2,000 calories. Lots of scrambled eggs, baked beans, toast, orange juice, peanut butter and coffee.

Whereas I probably should have started the week off light, I wanted to get a good head start just in case I encountered any setbacks during the week. The pack was uncomfortable and I spent many hours plodding around without anyone really giving a hoot about what I was doing. Many people thought I was just some idiot walking slowly. A few even told me this.

The bergen became incredibly uncomfortable, the weight was shifting backwards and I was having to lean forward and hunch my shoulders up with my trapezius muscles to try and keep the pack close to my back.

I ended the first day at 21.51km absolute shattered, exhausted and feeling very drained and disappointed that my efforts had barely raised any money for the charity.

I needed to sort my kit out, get a good night sleep and get ready for the next day.

Day 2 (Tuesday)

This morning I woke up feeling absolutely horrendous. My legs were incredibly sore, my hips, quads, and lower limbs in pain. I could not work out whether the pain I was experiencing on the lower parts of my legs were extremely sore calves or the herald of Achilles tendinitis. Alarm bells rang in my head. Had I undertaken this challenge too soon?

While I was eager to get this challenge completed and in a reasonably good time, I also began to worry that my Achilles could be wrecked beyond repair. Due to life commitments, I wasn't in a position to allocate a whole day to walking on day 2, which I guess in hindsight worked out well.

I prepped my meals, consumed an adequate number of calories and also fine-tuned my recovery nutrition for my return. I decided to attach a charity T-shirt to the front of my bergen and wrote in white Tipex "100kg / 100km". This was one of the best decisions I made as it allowed people passing to see what I was doing and get talking to me.

I set off and maintained a gentle plod around Cardiff. It was slow going. I gripped the straps with my hands, hunched my shoulders up and cracked on. By the end of day 2 I managed to achieve 7.2km which took me to a total of 28.71km.

Day 3 (Wednesday)

A little bit about me - I stopped drinking alcohol regularly in 2013, and aside from the odd special occasion haven't drank copious amounts of alcohol for some time. On the morning of day three however I woke up with what felt like a hangover from hell. I was well and truly knackered.

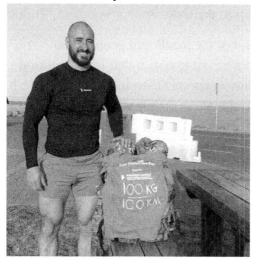

While my muscles were not as sore, I was so tired. I had a load of house work to get done, the food shopping, work and on top of that get these miles in. Today it was so tempting to take a rest day. But this is not what I wanted to do – I said I would carry the weight every day until it was completed.

I stepped out, put the ruck sack on my back and got plodding away. I had a lot of problems with my backpack on this day, the weight did not seem to be sitting correctly. In fact, I found that this air support bergen was not great for holding dumbbells as it was so wide and had a knack of pulling the weight backwards. This was never a problem I had experienced with the infantry bergen. But this was a trade-off I had to make. I feared the infantry bergen was simply not up to the task.

By this point, a lot of the locals and people who worked in the area began to notice that I was walking around Cardiff Bay every day carrying a heavy pack. I was stopped by quite a few people who were asking what I was up to. This was a very positive development as it meant that people were aware and making donations to the charity.

I am glad that I went with the option of doing loops around Cardiff Bay. I had considered doing different areas each day, or trying to walk a set distance point A to point B. Had I done that I don't think I would have got so much engagement and support from people who were living and working in the area.

By the end of day three I had travelled <u>33.74 km</u> in total.

Day 4 (Thursday)

I was excited for day four. This was the first day I was due to have any company on my walk. I had agreed to meet my friend Terry (founder of Rokman for whom I am a brand ambassador) at Cardiff Bay at 1000 and he would do an hour or so with me. Unfortunately, Tizzy (our special needs cat) decided to throw a spanner in the works.

It was the morning, and as I was prepping my food, kit, water and coffee for a long day of walking with weight. Tizzy decided she was going to poo all over the living room, jump in it, get it all over her paws and run it around the floor, sofa and try and climb the walls. I was so flipping tired and stressed out. I couldn't leave this all day to fester for Nez to come home to, so I spent a good 30-40 minutes cleaning up. Unfortunately, this meant I left quite a bit later than planned, hit traffic and was in a right foul mood by the time I met Terry.

I felt really bad for leaving him hanging around waiting for me but hopefully he accepted my explanation! Once all that was sorted, it was an easy start to the day. I'd done some foam rolling during my prep work and ascertained that it was indeed really sore muscles rather than Achilles tendinitis so that gave me a bit of a confidence boost to be able to get some extra distance in today.

I felt a lot stronger than I had done so far and having a bit of company certainly took my mind of it and made the kilometres feel quicker at least. I'd also begun to figure out different ways to rest the weight and was getting a bit more used to the air support bergen. I found that it was easier to just kind of prop the weight up on a bench or a bin rather than take the pack off. Carrying this kind of weight does reduce circulation to the arms as the straps put quite a bit of pressure on the shoulders almost like a tourniquet. Using this method, I was able to take the strain off, assist with the blood flow by shaking my arms out. It would also save me time. I did get quite a few funny looks when going into my rest positions. A few people thought I was dying, but I was being as strategic as possible with the rest breaks to keep the blood flowing to my arms, and to take the strain off my traps.

After Terry left, another good friend of mine, Steve turned up. He has been present at a couple of my challenges and is one of the most motivating people I know. He stayed with me for a couple of hours and I was very grateful for the time he spent with me. Day four became quite warm, and as I plodded into the afternoon solo my feet were oozing with sweat and I was getting very hot. Don't get me wrong though, it was beautiful weather and I was more than happy to be spending the day in the sunshine. For an extra challenge I added in some big hills after completing 10km or so. End of day four my total was <u>44.38km</u>.

Day 5 (Friday)

It was becoming apparent that I wasn't likely to achieve the 100km in seven days. I ran a few different scenarios in my head and for me to achieve it at my current rate it would have meant walking non-stop and pulling at least one overnighter. While the temptation was there to do this Saturday into Sunday, I reminded myself that I was not racing anyone and the goal was to complete this challenge and raise money for charity.

The better option would be to walk at busier times of day to get maximum exposure of what I was doing. This just so happened to be afternoon into the early evenings which was actually more convenient for me and also, I seem to be stronger in the afternoon.

The sunshine was bringing more and more people out and this meant I was receiving quite a bit of support and people saying they were going to donate. Some people recognised me from previous challenges and a few from my social media videos. At this point, I was feeling physically drained, but even with so much left to do I was undeterred and eager to finish this challenge. End of day five: 51.13km / 100km.

Day 6 (Saturday)

My body was slowly becoming less and less sore as it was forced to recover quickly and adapt to the demands it was being placed under. On day six I had company again. Steve popped down to see me for two hours and we had a lovely afternoon walking and taking in the beautiful seaside views at Cardiff Bay.

According to Steve I had made significant improvements to my stride and was walking a lot stronger than when he had seen me on day 4. I certainly felt stronger. I found at this stage I was strong whilst out and walking but during my down time I was just tired and certainly had no problem falling asleep. End of day six: 62.38 km / 100km.

Day 7 (Sunday)

Having scrapped the plan of pulling an all-nighter and finishing Sunday in a heap and knowing that I had a long day in work on Monday, I felt physically strong and my spirits were high. I'd broken the back of this challenge and the end was in sight. I was very excited to finish it, but I did not want my eagerness to make me over zealous. It was a marathon, not a sprint I kept telling myself. My girlfriend Nez came down to give me some support today for a couple of hours and she treated me to an ice cream which I really enjoyed during a break as we soaked in the sunshine. End of day seven: 72.53 / 100km.

Day 8 (Monday)

It was a bit unfortunate that today I was working in the gym and having to move a significant amount of gym equipment including weights and barbells around. It was a busy morning where I'd actually walked over 4km before noon just carrying gym equipment! (For the record: This was not sneakily added to my total).

When I returned home later that day, I had a small bite to eat and then got my kit squared away and headed off for my walk. I also wanted to test out my compression tights to see if they were of any use during the walk. They were.

Alan was meeting me on this day, he has assisted me with a couple of my challenges now and is a very supportive friend who I am lucky to have. It was another hot day and I just felt a bit drained, possibly due to the extra activity in work and not taking on enough calories during work. I had a change of strategy – I would count this as a rest day, do a very minimal amount of walking, go home, get carbed up with a large Domino's Pizza, get a decent night's sleep, and then have a full day on Tuesday and not stop until it was completed. At the end of Day eight I had walked 77.37km which meant that on Tuesday, I would need to walk 23km to achieve my goal.

Day 9 (Tuesday) "The Long Day"

As I prepped for day nine, I was going to refer to this one as "Hell Day". In fact, in my head, I was calling it this before I even started.

Reaching for my dry wipe marker pen I wrote down my game plan on the white board for the day. I calculated that I needed to walk 5.75km four times and that was it. Done. With that strategy in mind, I prepared my water bottles and my meals and set off.

The plan was to start off at around 11am and I was feeling as strong as an ox. Liaising with the Royal Brompton and Harefield Hospitals Charity, I informed them that I would be completing the challenge today and that I was going to throw everything at it.

This meant that I had plenty of calories on board – a large size Domino's pizza, hot freeze-dried meals that would be suitable for an expedition to the Antarctic, bananas, plenty of water, spare clothes, compression clothing lots of warm kit and plenty of water.

I had analysed all the data of the last weeks tracked walks and calculated that I would likely finish sometime between midnight and 2am.

The Royal Brompton and Harefield Hospitals Charity – who had been tracking my progress and supporting me the whole way dropped me a message asking me when I was likely to finish. Ever the optimist, I replied that I'd likely be finishing between 10pm and 2am.

Shortly afterwards I was contacted by their media department who had put together a press release to pass to the local journalists advising them that I was due to finish at 10pm if any of them were interested in attending!

This meant I had to go full steam ahead as how embarrassing would that have been if the press had turned up and I was still wandering around in the darkness with another 5km to go? I pictured this for a moment, chuckled and then cracked on.

But looking at my progress of the day, I was making really good time. My first 6km was smashed in two hours bang on. And I felt great. Knowing that I had to simply do four sets of 5.75kms I made sure the first two legs were longer than 5.75km while I was fresh knowing that legs three and four would be shorter and therefore easier.

After each leg I'd take a quick rest stop, my military training came into play and I had a slick routine:

- Sort my kit out

- Get my meal prepped

- Take boots off and get warm kit on

- Check my body for any issues

- Change socks

- Eat my food / rehydrate

- Drink coffee

- Dynamic stretches and quick re-warm up

- Warm clothes off

- Check kit – ensure water bottles are filled up

- Load kit onto my back and get going

I had become super self-sufficient. My process was fine-tuned and my confidence was up. I knew this was the end and I was feeling the strongest I had felt all week. The weather was beautiful (very hot) but to counter this I just needed to drink more water, knowing that my sweat would serve to keep my body temperature regulated.

People often say that with weather it can make or break you or whatever you are trying to achieve. While sometimes this can be the case, with preparation, training and the correct drills it doesn't have to be. Every different type of weather condition has the ability to cause a problem. We simply have to put in place steps to mitigate whatever that problem is and allow us to make the best of a given situation. I had learnt my lessons from previous challenges and began to remember my training from the Marines.

When doing loaded carries heat can be one of your worst enemies, as the heavy pack can restrict the body's ability to cool itself down; the rapid increase in sweat may cause dehydration, sodium loss and the core temperature can to rise to dangerous levels. It was not uncommon for military recruits to collapse during endurance marches with bergens on which is why we were trained to such a high standard in taking care of ourselves and also employing the buddy-buddy system; looking out for each other.

Over the last few days, I had become terribly efficient at resting, without taking the weight off me. The straps would restrict the blood flow and also sometimes make breathing difficult, or sometimes just needed to be readjusted for comfort. My rest position, would be a kind of crouch where I would support the weight with my legs and reduce the pressure off the shoulders. This looks a bit bizarre, but it was always a massive relief. However, some passer-by's thought that I was dying when I was in this position. At one point a young lad on a push bike cycled past me and yelled;

"Come on! You can do it brah!"

Which made me smile.

Within five hours I had clocked up 13km, my pace had improved and I still felt great. My body had adapted and the systems that I had employed were working to my advantage. One of the things I found that really helped was my decision to go with the compression tights.

Compression tights can help with circulation to the legs, but I feel it may have also been more of a placebo or some kind of psychological reassurance. Also, for some reason, when wearing these tights more and more people seemed to engage with me. I guess the general public are not used to seeing men walking around in white leggings! From people stopping to say, "Look at how big his legs are!" (a few were making a big deal about my glutes too!) then asking what I was up to, I'd feel great, my confidence would improve and on top of that I would be in conversation with someone who could potentially donate to the charity, and many said they would.

As the afternoon slowly descended into the evening. Nez turned up, which was a pleasant surprise for me. She stayed with me until the end. We were also joined later on by Alan and Steve.

My final rest stop was with precisely 4.02km left to walk. I was doing well for time, and what made this ideal was that for the first time I had assistance with my personal admin that needed to be completed on the rest stop. My biggest issue was my feet being in a lot of pain. And it was so nice just to take the weight off them while I instructed Nez on what to do to help.

We started the final leg as a small group. As the sun set and darkness descended over Cardiff Bay Barrage, I wanted to take my time and the target was to finish before 10pm. I was confident that this was achievable and looking at my split and pacing, I could easily do it before this. At a push I reckon I could have finished at 9.30pm. However, I wanted to enjoy this last moment and finish looking and feeling strong rather than hunched over and out of breath by walking at a fast pace.

I had planned the route to end exactly at the gate on the Cardiff Bay barrage where my car was waiting in the car park some 50 metres away.

I crossed the finish line at exactly 9.47pm as a small group of supporters clapped and cheered. After walking 23km carrying 100kg in under eleven hours I still felt great.

My immediate action was to start my procedure of unloading kit, taking my boots off and putting warm clothes on. A vehicle pulled up in the car park from the darkness and my friend Clive emerged holding a cup of coffee and dark chocolate nut bar. Unlike in my 2019 200lbs challenge – this was actually real and very well received.

Despite the rush to cross the finish line at 10pm in case the press was there… I can say that no reporters turned up. Despite this challenge being pretty brutal it seems the press only care if it's an odd object. Never mind, I had been updating social media as often as possible and also speaking with people who passed by helped with the fundraising efforts.

You may remember at the start I explained that I was going to call it "Hell Day". Why did I not keep that name? I changed it to "the Long Day" Here's the reason; I had built it up so high and prepared for it to be such a hard day that when I actually came around to tackling it, I was more than ready. It wasn't that bad after all, just a long slog that I broke down into 4 manageable chunks and I actually quite enjoyed this day although it was a relief to finally finish it.

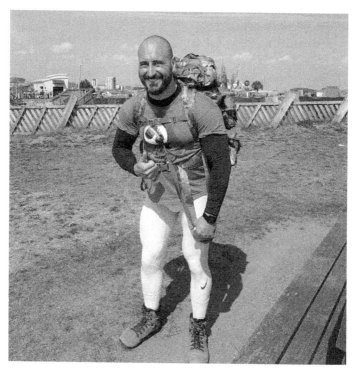

Fun Facts

My bergen was made to constantly weigh 100kg. I did not include water weight within this, as drinking it throughout the day would mean that at certain times, I could actually be carrying less than 100kg. The total weight would be 100kg + whatever water weight I was carrying. Having had many internet trolls scoff at my challenges in the past and say that I am cheating or taking parts out of the piano to make it easier, I was prepared to have my kit weighed at any time by anyone during this challenge.

In fact, no one I met ever doubted how much was in there, a few people actually had a go lifting the pack and putting it on their backs so they were able to experience what it was like to have a 100kg bergen on their back.

The air support bergen survived the nine day journey, however there is significant wear on the straps. I used a cam strap on the final day as a safety strap in case one of the bergens straps snapped whilst I was walking.

What I found amazing was how my body adapted during this challenge. On completion my muscles were not sore at all. My feet were but they recovered quickly. My muscles in my trapezius, calves and quadriceps were exceptionally tight however.

As muscles are worked hard, under heavy loads that they are not used to, the muscles fibres are damaged on a microscopic level. Providing there is sufficient rest and nutrition to recover, they will grow back bigger and stronger. Bioelectric Impedance Analysis of my muscles after this challenge showed that I had increased muscle mass in my legs at a rate similar to a progressive weight training programme. What it also showed was my left and right legs were perfectly balanced. Of course, following a structured weight training programme would be safer, easier and likely more effective in the long term for building muscle, but I did find this observation very interesting.

I was able to maintain speeds of 4kmph with 100kg on my back, yet I had no back lower pain whatsoever.

£1,250 raised for the Royal Brompton and Harefield Hospitals Charity. The Heart Vs Lungs challenge collectively was able to raise a staggering £29,278.

This challenge served as a firm reminder that, even though things may seem very daunting and nearly impossible at the start. With perseverance and consistency, the goal will be reached.

Which Challenge was the Hardest?

Which Challenge Was the Hardest?

One of the questions I often get asked is "what challenge was the hardest?" This is a difficult question to answer as they all presented different issues and were all difficult in their own unique ways.

The Triple Challenge was long, gruelling and smashed my whole body from different angles. Even my triceps were sore somehow! I think my body started finding alternative, unheard of ways to complete pull ups! Also, it's worth noting that I was inexperienced, ill-prepared and upon reflection I severely underestimated this challenge. The entire challenge was also completed 100% solo. But I learnt from my mistakes. This escapade taught me valuable lessons, many of which I already knew, but had forgotten.

The Car Pull Marathon was very tough at times, but depending on which stage of the track was also offset with some easy bits. I also had excellent support and thoroughly enjoyed this adventure.

The piano carry required the most physical, brute strength, and was relentless. But it was over relatively quickly - in three hours and what's more I trained for this one extensively, the pressure nearly got to me, but once I overcame that I genuinely enjoyed the event.

The 100kg over 100km required the most grit and endurance. This challenged me in ways that I have not been challenged before. Not only was this a physical challenge, it was mentally tiring and my organisation skills were tested. It was almost like doing the piano carry every day for nine days, but without the support. However, my body adapted, and I really enjoyed the final day, but was glad to see the back of this one!

It is certainly very difficult to compare things especially when they are months or years apart. It is also worth noting that I was in different physical condition for each challenge. So, I will leave it with this - the Car Pull Marathon and the Piano Carry I would love to do again if I ever had the opportunity. However, as far as I'm concerned, the Triple Challenge and the 100km can be confined to my memories and the pages of this book.

What I can say with conviction, is that I am glad I did all these challenges. Pushing myself outside my comfort zone and doing something significantly different to the norm is in my character and I am finally starting to embrace this, constantly learning as I go.

A few people have stopped me and told me that I will regret doing these things when I am older. That's probably very true. My body will probably be knackered. But could that also be from nearly five years in the Marines? Fifteen years of weightlifting? Seven years of running? Four years of sitting down in work for up to fourteen hours a day? Working shifts for most of my life? Partying hard and drinking copious amounts of alcohol in my youth? And equally so I could also be struck down in a freak accident or suffer some horrible disease. Our time on this earth is limited. We have one life and I would rather spend mine doing what I enjoy rather than as a caged tiger watching the world go by.

Lessons from the
Royal Marines

Lessons from the Royal Marines

If you are still reading you have probably begun to realise that the Royal Marines have had a massive influence on me.

I wanted to share some important lessons that I learnt particularly during recruit training that I found very helpful. I write these now because I am at an interesting stage in my life where I seem to be embracing physical challenges and putting myself out there more than ever before. I also find that I am now particularly interested in the psychological aspects and impacts of physical challenges.

This is causing me to remember things that I had all but forgotten and allows me to apply them to everyday situations or during the physical challenges that I have come to enjoy.

Many people reading this book may be interested in joining the Royal Marines or other elite military regiments. If that is the case then reading these may give you a head start into the mindset that is required to earn and wear the coveted Green Beret.

In my younger years I may not have recognised the value of these lessons, nor was I able to implement them into my life. It is only now, that I am beginning to understand the importance of what I learnt over sixteen years ago.

False Peaks

During endurance marches carrying heavy kit, we were often forced to march up long hills with horrendous terrain that seemed to go on forever. Our shoulders were sore, our legs ached, we were hot, tired, and exhausted. The training grounds picked by the military were excellent in terms of physical preparedness, yet torturous and could break a weak mind.

What made these hills so devilish were the notorious false peaks.

It is a very common tactic for an individual undergoing anything physically or mentally challenging to select goals, targets and end points. A certain round number on the treadmill or a target of reps in the gym. Often this target is something we can see or visualise. The top of the hill is a common one when undertaking this style of endurance march.

However, these routes are specially selected by the training team to cover terrain that includes false peaks.

Imagine the scenario; you are exhausted, fed up, cold, wet, and your feet are blistered, swollen and tender. Your legs are sore and your joints feel like the cartilage has completely worn away. Your breathing is rapid and your heart feels like it will burst out of your chest. You stumble on some uneven ground and the pain shoots through your ankle. The strap from the General Purpose Machine Gun you are carrying digs into your neck turning it red raw. The prickly heat stings like an army of ants are nibbling away at your back. Every part of your body hurts but you having to keep walking up this damn hill, and then…. you see the top.

It's only a few minutes away then it will level off. While you know you won't be able to stop, at least it will be easier and it'll give you a chance to recover.

As you get closer to the top the comfort begins to set in. Excited you step a little faster to get the relief that little bit sooner. And then. You see it. The top of hill is not the top at all, it plateaus briefly only to rise again to an even steeper hill with even worse terrain. This will happen again. And again. And again. Not over the period of a few hours but over a period of several days.

This type of training is designed to weed out the weak and those who survive it will build up stronger. We may think things are over, but we never know what is just around the corner. But stick with it, keep going and it will end.

Dislocation of Expectation

Another favourite tool employed by military training teams that is quite similar to the aforementioned false peaks is dislocation of expectation. This one however, is a lot more engineered than the above that relies on the natural landscape.

This psychological tactic will lure a recruit into a false sense of security, only to then flip things around into a world of discomfort. Cast your mind back to the previous scenario, you're out on a training exercise and this has been going on for the better part of five days and you know the exercise is due to end soon.

Tiredness sets in and you're struggling to stay awake as you march over the hill. You see the coach that transported you to the start of exercise in the distance. It is directly in front of you and you march towards it, ready for you to offload your kit, jump onboard and head back to camp for a shower, some hot food and some sleep.

It's getting closer and you're so relieved that this is over. If you're lucky, you may even get an hour or two of sleep on the coach! But then, your Corporal does not tell you to stop. You march straight past the transport and continue the exercise and the painful march.

This lesson is very similar to the False Peaks – you

may expect things to go in a certain way, you may be enjoying a comfortable environment, but life can quickly change and the heat in the pan can suddenly reach boiling point without warning. Dislocation of expectation prepares us for these scenarios and give us the tools to be able to mentally deal with them, come up with a strategy and survive.

This lesson was something that I certainly forgot about when I became a civilian. Life is like a roller coaster of ups and downs, but when we are going down it is very difficult to imagine that it will go up again. I have had to nose dive a few times to remember this lesson.

Importance of Hot Meals and Hot Drinks

The military literally employs people to be wet, cold and exhausted. As Royal Marines, that should have been in our job description. Hot food and drinks can really increase the performance of an individual, when out in the field or doing some tough physical challenge. Our bodies need it. I have witnessed (when serving with less disciplined regiments and also as a civilian) people completely "wrap" when they get cold and tired. (In the Royal Marines the word wrap means give up).

What happens is the individual, suddenly decides to stop looking after themselves. They decide that it's too much effort to cook their food, or make themselves a hot drink but this is a slippery slope downwards.

It is important to recognise this, the act of preparing the hot meal gives your mind a purpose, something to focus on and the hot meal will warm your body up and keep you going. A state of mind can quickly become negative, but we also have the tools to be able to recognise this and snap out of it.

It would be at this point that a typical Royal Marine would make a "hot wet" (what Marines call a hot drink) and laugh about how shit their situation is. The Royal Marines call this **cheerfulness in the face of adversity.**

Do Not Take the Easy Option

As a young man on my Potential Royal Marines Course, during the bottom field assessment we were being run ragged by the assault course. We were instructed to run through and over some obstacles. It was a cold winter day, the ground was muddy, wet and cold.

One of the obstacles is a long net, low to the floor that you crawl under. There are two nets both next to each other, one of the nets on the right-hand side was almost fully submerged with dark murky cold water. The net to the left, was nice and dry.

As the Physical Training Instructor barked at us to crawl under the net, I ran to the closest one – which happened to be the one with the murky water. While I considered the other option, I went with my gut feeling to go for the wet one. Two other potential recruits were hot on my heels, but went out of their way to go under the left one.

The instructor erupted with rage as I submerged myself in the ice-cold water and pushed forward through the large muddy puddle. I could hear him yelling at the others something about them not wanting to be wet and cold and that they weren't suited to be in the Royal Marines. As far as I am aware those individuals were not invited back to start recruit training.

This lesson always served as a reminder for me – that when presented with multiple options, the easy one is not always the best one and the journey that can be had by stepping outside of the comfort zone can certainly be more rewarding.

Failure is an Opportunity to Succeed

When I was approaching the end of Recruit training, I failed two of the Commando Tests. Luckily, you are allowed two attempts. But it meant I would have to attempt the Endurance Course again almost straight after the 9 Mile Speed March (Test 2) and then I would have to attempt the Tarzan Assault Course twice on the same day.

While I felt completely and utterly defeated after failing the Tarzan Assault course, I picked myself up, drank a load of Lucozade and ran it again a couple of hours later.

I passed both on the second attempts, but certainly made test week a lot more difficult than it needed to be. However, this meant that come the 30 Miler – the final Commando Test, I was more determined than ever to succeed.

Physical Fitness

One of the things I found most interesting about Royal Marines Recruit Training, was the fitness programme. It had been so carefully put together based on the experience of the Physical Training Instructors and through study of thousands of young recruits.

I enjoyed watching how my fitness improved and how my body adapted (or didn't adapt) to the stresses that I was being subject to. I feel I learned more about fitness purely from taking part in this training than I have ever learnt on any training course.

Autumn 2005
Royal Marines Recruit Training Exercise
Last Light

After a day of endless marching, carrying our heavy Bergens, we were eventually instructed by the training team Corporal that we would be setting up a troop harbour position. The Sun had not been visible throughout the day, it has been overcast with a never ending drizzle that soaked us to the core.

The last 45 minutes of marching has been through a dense wood block, and we had long succumbed to darkness. Tall trees lined either side of us as we walked in single file, the thick canopy provided some shelter from the rain.

Our task was to silently bed down here for the night, but as we were in the Commando phase of training, we had to dig shell scrapes for us to sleep in.

The selected harbour position was on the side of a hill, there was an abundance of trees to provide us with cover and also to help us secure our ponchos to create a make shift A-frame shelter.

I unclasped my fold-up entrenching tool from the rear of my webbing and thrust it into the muddy ground. My bivvy partner, a fellow recruit joined in and between us we had dug a hole approximately 1 foot deep, 7 foot long and 5ft wide. We probably should have gone a bit deeper but we were tired and desperate to sleep, we would only have a few hours kip at best.

As we unravelled our waterproof bivvy bags from our Bergans, the rain lashed a deafening barrage on the tree canopy above.

I took cover underneath the A-frame and sat in the shell scrape on top of my role matt, ready to begin wet and dry routine. (A process of removing your wet clothes, to put your dry clothes on for sleeping – when you get up the wet clothes are then put back on).

The rain water broke through the canopy and slammed down on the waterproof poncho above my head. It was holding firm. As I unbuckled my webbing belt, a torrent of water crashed down the side of the slope and began filling our shell scrape with muddy water.

I threw my sleeping bag into my bergen and got my entrenching tool out and starting digging a channel for the water to drain out of the shell scrape, while my bivvy partner got to work digging a drainage channel on the outside of our shell scrape to protect us from the flash flood.

After about 20 minutes of digging in the downpour, our efforts prevailed and the water was being diverted around our sleeping hole. We clambered back under the poncho. I could barely see my roll matt, it was covered in brown runny mud, and so was I.

Not knowing where to start, I sat on the roll mat and felt the cold mud seeping through the seat of my trousers. I reached for one my rear webbing pouches, unclipped it and pulled out my water bottle and quenched my thirst.

Seconds later, water came pouring back into our shell scrape and started filling up with water again.

"For fucks sake!"

My bivvy partner yelled. He was tired and frustrated.

We both got up and started digging our channels again, this time deeper.

Eventually we were able to get changed into our dry

clothes and settle down into our sleeping bags. It was lovely, comfortable, dry and warm. My rifle lay by my side, and my head rested on my webbing. My wet kit stashed away inside my bergen just outside my sleeping bag.

I closed my eyes and began to drift off to sleep.

"Fucking hell!" The annoyed voice of my bivvy partner woke me from my slumber.

I looked up and saw that the wall of the shell scrape had collapsed inwards and a small waterfall was engulfing our sleeping bags. I smiled at him, as I knew what we had to do.

We had to get out of our dry kit, stow them away and put our wet kit back on to deal with this. The last thing we wanted was for our dry clothes and sleeping bags to get wet. We began digging our channels again, to remove the water.

By the time we had finished, we managed about 1 hour sleep before we had to get up again to move position.

Lessons

Maintain a Sense of Humour
Sometimes life will throw everything at you to knock you down. Maintain a sense of humour and crack on.

In that situation, getting angry and frustrated was of no benefit to anyone. We were fighting against a perpetual wall of water, trying to defend our shell scrape that we had spent time and effort to construct. All we wanted to do was sleep.

Make the Most of the Comfortable Moments – But be Ready for Action

After being in soaking wet clothes all day, and being physically drained; getting into dry clothes and lying down in a warm sleeping bag away from the elements is the best feeling in the world. Unfortunately, it doesn't always last forever, and it makes getting out of it into the wet and cold clothes even more difficult. However, had we decided to stay in our sleeping bags, instead of leaping into action we would have been left with a wet sleeping bag and no dry clothes. This could be severely detrimental to us. Overriding our natural instincts to be warm and dry, meant we were sacrificing an hour or so in our sleeping bags to be able to maintain our system for the rest of the training exercise.

Overcoming Instinct

November 2006
Basra, Iraq

Following a very brief lull in the attacks on British military force in Iraq, the insurgents were picking up their offensive and launching daily assaults against British troops who were becoming besieged in Basra Palace.

Saddam Hussein's magnificent former palace had been turned into a base for the British Army. Fortifications has been erected around the 20-foot-high walls and British troops resided within the large rooms of the once-decadent palace; huddled up on mattresses and camp beds with 30-40 men per room.

The Palace is located along the Shatt Al-Arab River. This would have been absolutely beautiful for Saddam to enjoy when he was in power; for us however, it lay us wide open for sniper fire and rocket attacks from across the river.

It was nearly 4 years into Operation Telic, and it seemed that the majority of Basra wanted the British out. Attacks on the base had stepped up, the frequency and intensity of ambushes / road side bombs had increased.

On top of this, there seemed to be no leadership, or end game. We were poorly equipped, and there seemed to be no desire to resolve the situation and the hundreds of British troops stationed in Basra Palace were focussed on defensive operations.

Blast walls were erected to try and reduce the number of casualties from shrapnel and indirect mortar / rocket fire. These were highly effective, but didn't serve to counter the problem at the source.

Commanders had decided that operations outside of the Palace walls were too dangerous in vehicles on the roads and they had reduced the number of journeys being taken by road and helicopter due to the risk of them being shot down. This is why we were there.

We had been flown in under the cover of darkness. The Palace had a self-contained pontoon with a handful of Rigid Raiders at our disposal. We were to conduct patrols of the river, pick up intelligence assets from the ground for debriefing and serve as a taxi service between another British outpost up river.

I had looked forward to arriving at Basra Palace. We had been at the Airport for most of the deployment and not a lot was happening there. Aside from our missions to the Maysan Province, we spent most of our time just sitting in a very hot tent.

The Palace was where the action was. And also, I had heard stories of a local man who had set up shop in a little shack within the base selling very nice Romeo &

Juliet cigars to the British troops.

When we arrived, his shack was all shut up and remained so for the length of time we were there. I later found out he had been detained and executed by the insurgents; decapitated for trading with British soldiers and made an example of.

Another role was eventually found for us. We would also serve as a Quick Reaction Force (QRF) during the night in an attempt to counter the IDF attacks from the other side of the river. It had been determined, that insurgents were pulling up in pick up trucks, setting up mortars, blasting them into the palace and then driving off. They were using different locations each night, making it difficult to predict where they were going to be next.

Our standby rooms for the QRF were a couple of metal shipping containers situated next to the pontoon. Inside one, was a handful of camp beds for us to rest on and all our weapons and equipment. The walls were adorned with maps and charts of the area. Our job was to wait in there at a high state of readiness. We had a VHF radio set up, that we would take it in turns to monitor, 1 hour each. Squished inside this metal container like sardines, our only entertainment was a wind-up radio, a tin can to throw stones in and our sense of humour. If the call came in, we would have to be ready to go within 1 minute.

It was a quiet night. The Palace sat in darkness, and the faint hum of the radio played the hits of 2006 on the British Forces Radio Station.

Suddenly, there was an almighty roar that came crashing overhead as a rocket soared above us. I leapt off my camp bed and climbed into my helmet; trying to get myself as close to the floor as possible in what seemed like slow motion and awaiting the hot shrapnel to rip through my body.

That second felt like an eternity.

"This is it," I thought.

But the shrapnel never came. The rocket had landed in the water.

Seconds later, the air raid siren wailed across Basra Palace. The whistle of an incoming mortar soared into the base and exploded with a dull thud.

As black smoke bellowed from the base, we were already kitted up in our body armour, helmet, webbing, life jacket and weapons loaded and made ready.

At the sound of the air raid sirens, the entire garrison of soldiers at Basra Palace was sheltering behind blast walls. Everyone, except the Royal Marines of 539 Assault Squadron.

We were waiting out for the Operations Room to

dispatch us. They were hurriedly trying to triangulate the mortars base plate location. Eventually, a grid reference came through the radio and we sped out of the Palace onto the main waterway in our two Rigid Raiders.

I was positioned at the front of the first craft, my machine gun ready to take any threat head on. The Rigid Raiders skimmed across the waters of the Shat Al-Arab, illuminated only by moon light.

As we sped towards our target, approximately 2km up river; a large wrecked shipped jutted out of the water loomed directly in front of us from the darkness.

"Shit!" the Coxswain shouted, veering the Raider sharply to the right to avoid a head on collision, I gripped on to avoid flying off the boat and laughed.

The Coxswain, redirected our course and we continued. The Shatt Al-Arab was littered with wrecked ships, relics from the 2003 invasion. Once glorious looking vessels (including Saddam Hussein's Super Yacht), lay in ruins and used only by local fisher men (and eventually by the insurgents for Waterborne IEDs).

We arrived at the location, nicknamed "RPG corner" to find it was quiet, the attackers had long gone.

Updating the Operations Room on the radio, we were told to "wait out," before swiftly returning back to base.

Lesson

Instincts can be overridden. While the natural instinct in this situation is to take cover and hide, it was our job to go after it head on. We were unsuccessful on this occasion, but we were undeterred.

Remember The Moments

It was a sweltering hot day in the Persian Gulf. The Royal Navy Lynx helicopter had spotted a suspicious speed boat travelling from Iran to Oman. We were deployed to intercept.

Upon sighting us, the boat accelerated and a high-speed pursuit began.

As our RHIB (Rigid Hulled Inflatable Boat) launched itself through the waves, the engine screamed as is revved. We were slowly closing on the speed boat.

The Lynx was in pursuit and came down in front of the boat, the helicopter crewman waving frantically for the boat to slow down. The guys in the boat paid no attention and sped underneath the helicopter.

The chopper then turned around in pursuit of the

escaping speed boat, overtook it in the air, spun around and hovered in the boats course. It gradually lowered itself down towards the sea, its down draft pushing circular waves away from the below it.

Not knowing what to do, the speed boat continued its course, approaching the hovering Lynx, while we tried our best to gain ground. Still hovering, the helicopter tilted its nose down and the main rotor blades swept dangerously close to the surface of the water directly in the path of the approaching speedboat. This was a clear signal to stop if ever I saw one.

The boat, slowed and then swerved to change course away from the rotor blades. This caused it to slow down and allowed us to catch up slightly, we were now only 50 metres or so behind. Our RHIB crashed through the waves as we altered our bearing to match the speedboat.

It was at this point that is appeared the men in the speedboat threw something over board. Rather than stopping to check, we maintained course on the vessel and we powered through the water.

The Sea rippled, its crashing waves distorted by the wake of the speed boat, our RHIB and the helicopter downwash. I looked out to the Port side to see if I could see what had been thrown and noticed a Seagull perched on a small piece of drift wood. It was listing heavily from side to side and he was just sat there, calmly observing the chaos around him. Time seemed to slow down as I locked eyes with this bird.

Then – I was back to it. The RHIB crashed over a wave and we gained further ground on the speedboat. One of the men turned to face us and the Sergeant gestured clearly with his arm to slow down. The man smiled and waved and then continued his course.

We caught up with the boat, came up alongside about 10 metres away and I raised my rifle up and took aim toward the speed boat. The man on the boat looked at me. The Sergeant gave his last warning. The man, who I assume thought he was about to be shot put his hands up and the boat slowed down (I wouldn't have shot him as there was no risk to life at this point). The boat's blue hull bobbed up and down with the chops of the wave.

The helicopter circled overhead and we pulled ourselves alongside the speedboat to speak with the men and search their boat. They were smuggling Eagles across the water who were all wrapped up in sheets to try and protect them from the blistering sun. It is not clear what had been thrown overboard and we were unable to locate it afterwards.

As we returned, the seagull was still there, relaxing on his piece of drift wood in the middle of the ocean.

Lessons

For me, this story serves to highlight that while we are going about our thing – life is moving on around us and it doesn't hurt to look around and take notice of the little things going on; as with the seagull and I, it may serve to make you smile in decades to come.

A Close Encounter

Royal Marines are amphibious soldiers, we specialised in beach assaults. That means we need to train in the sea and practice the different techniques of tackling the beach.

One of these is Surf Drills. Whilst nothing to do with surf boards, it would involve us riding the waves on our RHIBs and practising disembarking onto the beach in a tactical manner.

What better place to do this, than Machrihanish – one of the best surfing locations in Scotland!

We were wearing our ISBO suits (Immersion Suit Boarding Operations) which I had a particular disliking to. It was really big, cumbersome and I could hardly move in it. It felt like I was walking around with a pair of diving fins on my feet. I personally preferred the FRIS (Fire Retardant Immersion Suit) as this has a better fit, although it meant your boots and feet would get wet. The ISBO would actually wrap over the boots.

I wasn't in a position to debate what suit to wear, I was told to wear my ISBO, so I brought my ISBO.

We attached our day sacks using carabiners to the hull of the boat and launched our RHIB into the sea from the beach. We waded in and clambered into the boat.

We practised our drills, we would approach the beach as speed, before clambering out and assaulting an imaginary enemy position on the beach. Directing staff would provide feedback and then we would reset and repeat into the afternoon.

The waves at Machrihanish did not disappoint. It was particularly exciting to power over the wave and get air time on the boat before crashing down at speed.

As we were returning back from a successful assault rehearsal on the beach, the coxswain completely misjudged the waves. He spun the boat to side as a huge wave emerged from the sea. I looked up to a wall of water.

"Oh shit," the coxswain realised his error as we all gripped onto the inside of the hull.

The wave came underneath the boat, throwing us into the air and flipping us upside down. I am not sure what happened to the rest of the team as I was on the forward section of the boat and it smashed down on top of me as it hit the sea, disorientating me.

The RHIB was still being battered by the waves and my ISBO suit became tangled up in the daysacks that had been attached to the hull of the boat.

We practiced capsizing boats regularly; the drill is for everyone to go underneath the boat and come up alongside, number off to check everyone is there and then one man goes underneath, clings on while the others stand on the bottom, and pull back on a line to right it. The rest of the team were performing the earlier stages of this drill but I was caught underneath the boat. Every wave caused the RHIB to raise and then push me back down underwater.

I can only describe it as how I imagine being in a washing machine would feel.

I tried desperately to free myself, my head was being pushed underwater by the rubber bow of the boat and the handful of daysacks. I couldn't see a thing other than the murky water and bubbles. I had to change my tactic. I kicked down with my legs and they came into contact with a bit of ground. Luckily the water here was now only about 5 ft deep.

As the boat bashed down on me again, my head was forced underwater. I couldn't breathe and I pushed down with my feet as hard I could and squatted the front of the boat up until my head was above the water. I took a deep beath; now I had some control over this boat I managed to free myself from the tangled-up daysacks and pushed myself back away from underneath the RHIB, emerging next to my fellow Marines alongside.

"You OK?" One of them said.

"Fucking hell! Yes," I replied. Then we proceeded with the drill to right the boat.

Lesson

Take Action

What should have happened in this scenario, was something that I had done countless times before. I should have just been able to swim underneath the boat and then come up to surface outside the boat. But by some fluke I had found my ISBO had got caught up in a load of daysacks and I was getting smashed about by a rather large boat.

This meant that my relied upon technique was not working and no matter how many times I tried to swim under the water it just simply was not happening.

The whole encounter took place over about 15-30 seconds. This is enough time for panic to set in. But we need to remember that we are in control. Had I allowed myself to panic I could have ended up in a worse situation and could have swallowed water or even drowned.

My team were around me, and when they noticed I wasn't with them I imagine they would have come to my assistance. Although I was not prepared to wait and see how long it would take for them to come and help. I managed to summon the strength to be able to shift the boat in the air and find an alternative route of escape.

We can't achieve our goals by just coasting along through life. To make things work we need to take definitive action and direct out force to make things change. Sometimes we get stuck in a process of just repeating the same thing over and over again; expecting different results. When things don't work or go according to plan, assess the situation and don't be afraid to change tactics and take decisive action.

Exercising
Anywhere

Learning the Ability to Exercise Anywhere

I wanted to add this here as part of this book for a few reasons. As I write this section, during 2021, lockdown measures in the UK are being eased and gyms and leisure centres are being opened.

It reminds me of times in my life where I have had to keep fit and not had access to the gym. During my time in the Royal Marines where we were often stationed in the middle of nowhere but were required to maintain a high level of fitness. In the desert or on ship with minimal equipment, we certainly had to be fairly creative and motivated with our workouts.

However, I learned that you can certainly achieve a fantastic level of fitness and a great physique with just bodyweight exercises and running. There are plenty of conversations these days surrounding mental health and the ability of physical fitness to impact positively on our mental health, and during my time as a Marine when we were training hard daily, I felt great. Doing shuttle sprints on the flight deck of a warship in the open air and sunshine, felt amazing.

Saying that, just doing bodyweight exercises is not ideal and certainly not for everyone. From a wellbeing perspective it's great and also training outdoors is certainly very positive and healthy. We did use weights and equipment in our circuits a lot of the time and we also had access to weights, barbells and dumbbells on occasion.

During the national lockdown in the UK, we were allowed to go outside and exercise once a day. After a few weeks this was increased to be able to go out and exercise as many times as we liked during the day. Imagine how much more challenging this would have been if we weren't allowed outdoors at all?

When I worked as a Maritime Security Consultant between 2011-2013, I really had to think outside the box to be able to maintain my fitness routine. Our job back then was to embark upon a client vessel in an area of safety, whilst they were heading towards and through the designated high-risk area (at the time was a large portion of the Indian Ocean).

As armed security advisors, we had to fully lock the ship down and would spend days welding barricades and wrapping razor wire around certain areas of the vessel to make it difficult for any pirates to board the ship, and also restrict their movement around the ship if they were successful in boarding.

This also meant crew movement was restricted, and everyone was more or less confined to their cabins aside from meal times or to conduct essential work. Any movement on the upper deck would have to be authorised by the Officer on Watch in the Bridge and the Security Team would be advised. We couldn't have people wandering around on the upper deck if we came under attack for example. If we were monitoring suspicious looking skiffs in the area, authorisation would be denied.

While this job does sound very exciting and looking back it was certainly one of the best jobs I have ever had, the day-to-day life of a Maritime Security Operative on ship was certainly far from thrilling. Once the initial risk assessment, fortifications, preparations and subsequent training of the crew was completed, it was a case of watching and waiting. In the two years I did this role I only ever saw a handful of pirates and due to our vigilance, drills and procedures those I did see never made it closer than 300 metres from our ship.

The rest of the time was spent stood on the Bridge Wing staring out to sea at nothing but waves looking for pirates for up to twelve hours a day. We would study the radar, listen to radio transmissions and keep up to date with the latest security and intelligence reports to compile our threat assessments so we could advise the captain. The rest of it we were confined to our cabins that were no bigger than a garden shed; that often would be shared with someone else.

Sometimes the ship would break down, and we'd be left floating about in the sea, sitting ducks until the engineers managed to fix the problem and we'd limp away to continue our voyage. Other times, due to some international disagreement our ship would be denied entry into port and we'd be stranded a few miles off shore waiting for some people in offices thousands of miles away to decide what to do with us, as we slowly ran out of food.

On several occasions our lives were left in the hands of Poseidon, The God of the Sea as he sent humongous waves to batter our ship, throwing us from side to side like we were stones in a tin can being kicked about by a mob of playful youths.

There have been a few occasions in my life where I have genuinely thought I was about to die. One of them was on a particularly unseaworthy ship as we passed through what Portuguese mariners of the 15th

Century used to call the "Cape of Storms," near South Africa. I left my cabin to make a late-night cup of tea. As I stepped cautiously along the outside walk way, I approached the galley and suddenly my world turn upside down and I was forced to cling onto a metal pole with all my might as the ship listed sharply to side with the walkway disappearing into the dark sea.

On another occasion, passing through a rather large cyclone, I distinctly remember gigantic walls of water crashing over the upper deck and superstructure. This was life at sea. We were locked down and we could do nothing about it. We got on with our job, looked after each other, made the best of it. Tough times and shared hardships can make or break a person. With the right attitude and mindset these situations can strengthen our resolve.

One of the benefits of working in the maritime industry is I got to travel, see the world and experience different cultures. On my trips I saw exceptional wealth, juxtaposed with even more exceptional poverty. The fact of the matter is, no matter how tough I thought I had it, there was always countless people more worse off. And for me, I knew it was only temporary.

This is why I hoped that when the national lockdown was announced in the UK, it would serve as an opportunity for society to toughen up. An occasion for us to learn how to take responsibility and make use of the tools we have to improve our mental and physical strength / wellbeing. A moment for us to slow down and enjoy life. A chance for us to forget about things that are not really important. Re-evaluate our priorities and focus on our own personal health, the wellbeing and respect of others and our responsibility to the environment. A shot for us to stop complaining about the things we haven't got and spend our time enjoying the things that we have got.

While a lot of people have certainly gotten stronger and developed their character – many just seemed to have increased their ability to whinge, about anything and everything.

One of the things that made life at sea enjoyable was my fitness routines on board these ships. I would conduct bodyweight exercises during my down time on the floor of my cabin, or sometimes in engine compartments, where I could do pull ups from bulk heads. It was hot, with no air conditioning or comforts, it was tough but I got used to it. I purchased some resistance bands, so that I had a portable gym with me at all times. I'd do calf raises whilst I stood on watch looking out over the ocean. The fact is you just need a small amount of space and right attitude and you can train just about anywhere.

Workout Information

Workout Information

I wanted to share some of my lockdown workout routines to serve as a reminder to me and maybe give anyone reading this some ideas should they find themselves in a situation like this again. Here are some good practices to consider for anyone embarking on a fitness programme:

All workouts must begin with a thorough warm up. Remember the acronym **RAMP**, and follow this procedure:

Raise blood flow, muscle temperature, core temperature, muscle elasticity through low intensity movements

Activate & Mobilise your muscles and joints with dynamic movements

Potentiate the movements you are doing in the workout, e.g., gradually increase the weight you are doing on a squat, or build up speed on short sprints

Hydration

It is imperative that you stay hydrated throughout the day by drinking plenty of water. The easiest way to stay on top of this is to check the colour of your urine. Ideally it should be clear or a pale yellow. If it's dark yellow you need to drink more water. Make sure that you have drinking water with you during your runs, circuits, weight training or loaded carries.

Safety / Spatial Awareness

When walking, running or hiking; You are responsible for your route selection. It is advisable to select a route that is adequately lit, with good firm flooring and does not involve you going out on the road. You should wear high visibility clothing and appropriate training attire at all times. When going on a run / loaded march you should make others aware that you are going out, what you are doing, where you are going and an estimated time of return. Be aware that when out walking, cycling or running wearing head phones or earphones may be motivating, but it also limits your senses to any dangers such as vehicles or potential attackers. As a personal rule I never do this as I like to be aware of my surroundings at all times.

Injuries / Feeling Unwell

Pushing through a workout when you're injured or unwell is not smart and injuries are not a badge of honour. If at any point you feel unwell or become injured during a training programme you must stop immediately, contact your doctor and not resume the programme until you have had permission from a medical professional.

This train line represents your journey through a training programme:

If you get injured for whatever reason you must stop, it is simply like getting off at a stop and waiting for your next train to continue your journey.

Once you are ready to continue your journey then it is a good idea to start off a little bit further behind as you will have lost some of your gains and this will give you the opportunity to build back up.

It's very important to accept this process. Many a trainee has fallen victim to not allowing their body to heal for being concerned about not achieving their fitness goals. The longer and harder you train on an injury the longer it will take to recover. You will not be able to perform at your potential if you are limping around in pain. Stop, rest, recover, rehabilitate and get going again.

What's also equally important and often overlooked is reflection. And I'm not talking about checking yourself out in the mirror. If you develop an injury, then it is a wise idea to try an understand how this happened. What led to this happening? If the injury is a result of direct blunt trauma (such as a sports injury) it doesn't take a detective to figure out the cause, but don't always take the apparent reason at face value.

A lot of injuries occur due to a build-up in poor training practices, tight, weak or imbalanced muscles. These injuries may sometimes manifest themselves when doing something seemingly harmless such as picking up an object from the floor or putting on your trousers.

Once you identify how and why the injury occurred then use this as an opportunity to put steps in place to prevent it from happening again.

I learnt the hard way. One summer many years ago I decided I didn't want to skip a gym session that I was not ready for. Having partied to the early hours of the morning celebrating my friend's birthday - drinking copious amounts of alcohol and getting next to no sleep I went straight into a long shift at work.

At the time I was a door supervisor and was doing security for a very busy event. Much to my annoyance the air conditioning had packed in on one of the hottest days of the year. Dressed in a suit I was sweating profusely and fighting with intoxicated punters.

When I got home that night, I noticed I was suffering mild symptoms of heat illness. Not a problem at the time – I was trained to recognise this and dealt with it, then I went to bed. The next day was my day off. I knew I wasn't 100% but decided to hit the gym for what was scheduled to be an intense squat session. In my head I proposed that I would just do a light workout and continue my schedule in a couple of days. Fate however, had other arrangements for me.

Upon arrival at the gym, I was filling up my water bottle at the water fountain when the hottest girl in the gym appeared out of nowhere and decided to engage me in conversation. The macho man in me quickly quelled the idea of performing a light weight workout… I didn't want to look like a wimp so I marched over to continue my heavy session – neglecting my warm up.

During my second set of squats, I gripped the bar, took a deep breath lowered myself down and as I was about to push up felt an intense explosion in the back of my head. My vision blurred and experienced an excruciating pain that was worse than any kick or punch to the head I have ever sustained. Me being me, I continued my workout, and subsequent sessions after that for two weeks. However, during these two weeks I experienced blinding headaches, memory loss and slurring of words.

Eventually I gave in and went to see a doctor, I had sustained a brain injury and had to take six months off training or any physical activity that could raise my blood pressure. Upon returning to the gym my muscles had become weak and I ended up pulling my adductor magnus as it had become tight. The outcome of this story is; Rather than skipping one session I forfeited over 6 months, and then had to rehabilitate secondary injuries. What I learnt from this:

- I let my ego get the better of me which probably made the damage even worse

- I never skip a warm up – if anything I warm up too much now

- I will only train when I am ready to train

- I stopped drinking alcohol (apart from the odd special occasion)

This harsh lesson is not only applicable to an injury. I had to analyse what went wrong and how I can prevent it happening again. This process can be applied to any situation or scenario to dynamically assess performance and improve over time.

Come up with a plan, **Execute** the plan, over time, **Analyse** the results and then **Adjust** the plan based on feedback.

It is a continuous cycle of perpetually striving to improve in any target area.

Performance
Mindset

Performance Mindset

While physical training is crucial to your success, an often-overlooked aspect of a fitness programme is mindset. If you have got a weak mind, or are simply not in the right frame of mind throughout it is unlikely you will be able to perform to your full potential.

You will often hear people state that they are "bringing their A-Game", "Getting in the zone" or "putting their war face on"

These are sayings depict the mental transition someone is taking to allow them to perform at their best.

Here are some mindset approaches that can be used to increase your performance in fitness, sport, work or life in general.

Focus

Divert your attention to one thing and be disciplined about it (for example, improving your run time). Focus your mind on solely thinking about improving your running - hitting that sub 9 1.5 mile run time (or whatever your aim is).

When I had fitness goals, I was thinking about them so hard I was even dreaming about them. When I wanted to be a better runner, I'd be running in my head even on my days off training, I was thinking about running. When I was trying to build my muscles, I was doing bench press in my sleep (much to the annoyance of who I was sharing a bed with at the time).

If you're easily distracted or sitting about playing on your phone all evening and not thinking about your goals, you will be lacking the focus to move onto the next step.

Visualisation

Imagine doing the activity over and over in your head like you're obsessed. When I was training to carry the piano up a mountain it wasn't new for me when I got to the top because I'd already been there. I'd walked the whole route with an imaginary piano on my back. I knew the steps I had to take. I prepared so well for this challenge that on the day, everything went exactly as I had visualised.

I'll let you in on a little secret, I even started writing the **Piano Carry** chapter of this book before I had even acquired the piano. Research has shown that writing down your goals increases the likelihood of them being achieved.

Make a Start

Some days you feel lazy and rubbish. It's a fact. I don't care who you are, every single one of us has days where we just cannot be bothered to train. I have been there on countless occasions. Most days, I feel like that. THESE ARE THE DAYS THAT COUNT.

If you feel this way just get up put your trainers on and make a start. Commit to doing just a warm up, mobility session, short walk or gentle jog. Once the blood is flowing that focus will return. I will add a note to this, if you are completely overworked, ill or injured this rule may not apply, then it is best to rest and recuperate. You will have to be the judge of that.

Recognize Your Achievements

We all like a win. Knocking one second off your time is a victory, so celebrate it. Multiple wins will set you on a roll to success.

Remember Why You Are Doing This

This is a powerful tool to have in your arsenal. It can link in heavily with the visualisation principle as mentioned earlier. When I was working shifts and training towards a bodybuilding goal, I remember sitting on the bench press tired, flat, unmotivated and the weight feeling heavy. In my head I would visualise my goal and think about why I was doing this, I'd move my arms, push them out to the front, swing them across my chest, tense the muscle – whatever to get the blood flowing through them, lie down and smash out a heavy set.

Marginal Gains

Every single thing you do is one small step towards your goal. These incremental improvements may seem insignificant in isolation but when added together becomes a snowball effect. I call this the **100% Principle** – Of all the serious challenges I have attempted, trained and prepared for – the goal of completing this was assigned the value of **100%** and all my efforts contributing towards the goal were assigned % value to take me towards that goal.

For example; on a fat loss journey each gym session you make, each step you take throughout the day, every time you opt for the stairs instead of the elevator, each time you turn down a cake or a chocolate bar it all adds up. Individual things can be seen as nothing, but they are all very important and they add up.

I had very little time to train for the car pull marathon, so I made sure that my footwear was adequate, the tyres were inflated to the correct pressure and I had trained, practiced and practiced. All of these things, and the procedures I put in place got me as close to the 100% mark as I could within the allotted time.

Flip the Switch

Physically make the mental transition in your mind. Press the button inside your brain that activates the

Beast Mode. It's the primal bit inside of us and a method that soldiers have to employ during close quarter battle to gain and maintain the upper hand – Violence of action.

Imagine the scenario. Armed gun men have taken over a building and are threatening to kill innocent civilian hostages. Negotiation efforts have failed and the only option left on the table is to attempt to storm the building.

There are two ways a soldier can try and breach this building. They can bimble up to the door, open it, stroll in and then get shot to pieces by the enemy hiding in the corner of the room.

Or they can sneak up to door, and without warning violently smash / blast it open, immediately launch flashbangs into the room to disorientate the enemy whilst a swift stream of highly trained troops rapidly and aggressively gain entry; providing overwhelming force until the enemy is neutralised and the hostages are saved.

In this scenario, both groups of soldiers were attempting the same thing – to gain entry into a room with a bad guy in. The difference was how they went about it, the second group flipped the switch; one mine they're nice guys and then their war face goes on.

In Recruit training they used to get us to practise this against dummies, we would smash them to pieces with our bayonets. If we didn't get aggressive enough, we would have to go again, and again.

We can apply this same transition method to our daily lives – too tired to hit the gym? Flip the switch. Struggling to hit your goals and targets? Then flip the switch and become what you want to be.

I even went as far as getting the words "Beast Mode" written on my training shoes. If I'm not feeling up to training hard then after putting those shoes on I can't train half-assed!

Step Out of Your Comfort Zone

This was the hardest thing for me to do in my younger days. I was so afraid of failure, afraid of looking stupid. Because I trained hard and was in good shape and had a bit of an ego, I was so concerned about what other people would think if I failed something that on some occasions I wouldn't even try if I suspected I wouldn't be very good at it. The point is… I never tried.

Enjoy the Journey

Our lives constantly change. What are goals now in years to come will be just memories. What you experience on your journey will have a more lasting impact on your character than the results.

Lockdown
Workout

My Lock Down Workout

Here is a circuit training routine I would complete during the lockdown. Equipment carried:

- Military bergen (to carry the kit)

- Walking boots (worn during transit)

- Trainers (worn during workout)

- 2 x dumbbells (20-30kg dumbbells)

- Roll mat

- First aid kit

- Water bottle (1 litre)

- Gloves

- Sunglasses

- Sun cream

- Camera tripod

- Resistance bands

After a 2 mile or so hike carrying the equipment, I would put the kit down, take my boots off and put my trainers on. Then begin with some light gentle jogging, mobility drills, dynamic stretches and a short series of sprints.

(Warm up followed the **RAMP** procedure)

Weighted Burpee x 10 - 20

Dumbbell Clean and Press x 10 – 30

Shuttle sprint x 2

Press ups x 12 – 25

Bent over row x 12 – 25

Burpee x 20 – 50

Shuttle Sprint x 2

Mountain climber Press Ups x 10–20

2 – 3 rounds depending on how much time I had.

Stretches, followed by a 2-mile hike carrying the equipment.

The Little Chapter
of Challenges

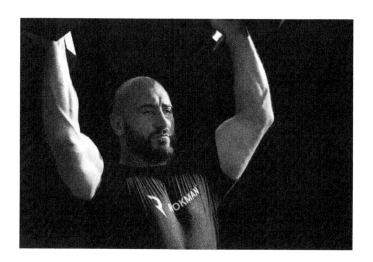

The Little Chapter of Challenges

While the previous challenges mentioned at the start of this book were some of my best physical achievements in the last two years. I always referred to them as "Big Challenges".

A big challenge to me is something that requires a lot of effort, commitment and focus. One thing that I really think about and put my mind to doing. Along the way I have also enjoyed participating in little challenges.

Little challenges are physical efforts that I spend very little time preparing for (often no training whatsoever) and are performed merely for fun and for the experience. I care very little if I "pass" or "fail" these challenges. Often, they are things that are well away from my comfort zone and this adds to the fun of it.

These little challenges are usually over in a few hours and I'll do them on my day off or at the end of my session.

Here are a few of my favourite challenges that I have undertaken in recent years:

Drown Proofing

The name itself sounds like an absolutely horrendous experience, but this had got to be one the most exciting things I have ever tried! I tried as best I could to simulate the Navy SEAL's Drown Proofing test which involves jumping into a 3.5-metre-deep pool with your feet tied and hands bound behind your back.

When the SEALs do it, they have a load of safety divers. It is dangerous, so I really do not recommend anyone go out and try this. Following an interesting conversation with the manager of a swimming pool as I explained what I was intending to do… the pool was all mine for an hour!

Please note – I did not have my hands and feet firmly bound with rope as I did not have safety divers. I had looped rubber bands around my wrists and ankles which would give me a little pull if I started using my legs or if they came apart. But if I needed to – I could have broken loose with ease.

With 2 very professional life guards on standby I jumped into the pool to begin my favourite part… the surface bobs. This is something I had wanted to try since I was a kid. I read up on it in some magazine so you can probably imagine how excited I was to actually be trying it out!

The surface bobs are more a test to see if you can keep your cool. If you panic it's all over! You quite simply have to sink down to the bottom of the 3.5-metre deep pool and when your feet touch the bottom push up so your head comes to the surface, take a breath of air and then sink back down to the bottom.

When I was a kid, I swear I read that this had to be done for 20 minutes, and I thought "that sounds solid!" However, upon research it seems I must have mis-read as in actual fact it has to be completed 20 times. Although you are not allowed to hang around at the surface, it's a quick breath and then straight back down.

While this all sounds easy enough, as I tried to sink down, I began to realise that I just floated in the middle of the water, dropping from the surface but not really making my down to the bottom in any hurry.

This is where the confidence comes in; the ability to override the natural sense of panic. Panic can set in very quickly. Once the correct technique had been learnt, it just became a case of repeating, sinking to the bottom pushing up with the legs so my head reached the surface of the water, taking a deep breath and then allowing myself to sink while exhaling.

I found this so relaxing and enjoyable that if I had my own personal 3.5-metre-deep pool I would certainly add this to my daily routine after work!

The 40 Miler

June 2020. In the middle of lockdown, the UK had just had its sunniest month on record. All my fitness training had taken place outdoors and I was going through a phase of trying various fitness tests inspired by armed forces from around the world. This seemed to be quite popular with others as well and numerous people were attempting the British Army Fitness test or other relatively easy tests.

I decided to up the ante somewhat and attempt a test inspired by the Delta Force final selection test "The Long Walk". This would involve carrying 56lbs + water on my back (total starting weight was 67.8lbs) over a distance of forty miles within a time limit of fourteen hours.

For this fun challenge I was accompanied by my girlfriend Nez. As we set off from Cardiff Bay on foot, we were graced with the most beautiful sunny weather that made this start quite enjoyable (although very hot and sweaty!)

The weight was not a problem, and the distance wasn't too bad, but as we approached the half way pointed I noticed that we were going a bit slower than I had planned. Nez, realising that I was getting a bit irritable about our slow pace ended up having a nap in a field so I could run off ahead to make up the time and pick her up on the way back!

Typical of the Welsh weather system, as we passed the half way point the blistering heat made way for several hours of intense torrential rain. Making us even more determined to finish Nez and I got back to Cardiff Bay completing the forty miles in the allowed time (although the terrain was far easier than what I imagine the actual Delta Force do).

I was very proud of Nez for completing an ultramarathon that day, with no notice or preparation.

We enjoyed it that much we have discussed making this an annual challenge!

100 Rep Challenge

This was short, sharp and harder than I expected. Quite simple really – get 2 dumbbells weighing 25kg each and work through 100 reps. Just keep churning the reps out until 100 is completed as quickly as possible. I can't remember if it started raining during this workout or if I was just sweating that much... but steam was certainly coming off me by the time I finished this cheeky little challenge!

1000 Burpees

In my younger years I always remember burpees being a tough exercise. We would usually do sets of around 20-25 and rarely much more. I remember being made to do 500 "Bastards" in Royal Marines recruit training and they're a similar exercise, but never did I think I'd do 1000 for fun. This one is a grind. I picked the original old school burpee (The burpee was invented by Dr Royal H Burpee – and it did not include a press up or a jump). It took around 90 minutes for me to complete this workout. It's a good personal challenge that would be achievable to most people and I believe is a great developer of mental toughness.

500 Burpees

This is the little brother of the 1000 burpee challenge. I tried this one first. It was a tough one, I opted for the version including a press up and the challenge was completed in around 40 minutes – less than an average gym work out! Knowing that I could achieve 500 burpees, meant that I knew I could do 1000, simply by doing 500 twice.

Rock Climbing in Spain

One of my earlier challenges involved heading to Spain. While most young brits were disembarking the plane at Malaga to go partying, I met up with some local climbing instructors for an intense climbing session in the mountains.

This was an absolutely amazing experience. I spent three days in a beautiful little village at the base of the mountains and attempted some intermediate climbs.

Some of these routes were quite tough, and I received excellent instruction and quickly learnt that it was not always the best idea to just try and pull up these rocks with brute strength!

Technique is very important, using the legs and thinking ahead to find the ideal foot hold to push off with was the best strategy! While I was no way in the same league as the instructors, I was certainly a better climber by the time they were finished with me!

The Haunted Lake

In February 2020, I decided it would be a brilliant idea to undertake a challenge in the Brecon Beacons mountains. Part of the challenge would involve swimming across Lyn y Fan Fach – a lake up in the

Welsh mountains. It was a particularly cold day; heavy snow had fallen and it was -8°C with an icy wind that made it feel even colder.

Lyn y Fan Fach is located 500 metres above sea level; is recognised as one of the coldest lakes in the country and is 29 metres deep.

Geology aside, the lake is also connected to folklore legend and it apparently haunted by a spectre known as the Lady of the Lake.

Arriving at the side of the lake early, I stripped down to my under pants and walked into the icy water.

Scrambling over uneven rocks, the cold water ripped against my legs. I proudly marched in, as if offering myself as a sacrifice for the Lady of the Lake.

I leapt forwards into the water and started swimming, a powerful breast stroke.

The cold water felt great against my skin, and in the mountain air it was very refreshing. I got about half way across the lake and things changed.

The water was a lot colder than I had anticipated. The air turned silent, my breathing turned into a pant and my arms and legs began to go numb. My heart was pulling blood away from my limbs to try and protect my internal organs. But I needed my limbs to be able to swim to shore.

My powerful breast stroke swiftly turned into a feeble doggy paddle. I began to gasp for air. My body was telling me to rest. I don't float well so I needed to keep paddling. I could sense the depth of the lake below me. It felt as though I was being beckoned to stop, give in and just allow myself to sink.

I was swimming on a bearing towards a piece of land that had been directly opposite me. I kept focussing on that, but considered turning around. I guessed I was half way across but I wasn't sure. My concern was that if I stopped and turned around, I'd lose my momentum and it would have been crushing if I was past the half way point and had to turn around again. I needed to keep moving. I was spluttering and my chest was tight. It was like my entire throat had closed up and I had no strength in my arms or legs. I flapped them around as best I could in an uncoordinated paddle.

There was a bit of land to the right of my target that appeared a little closer. I altered course slightly to try and reach this. I knew the dangers of hypothermia and swimming in cold water and realised I had only seconds left before I could be incapacitated.

The cold water engulfed me, my breathing was shallow and I sputtered water away from my mouth. My hips began to sink down towards the bottom of the lake as if being pulled down by some magnetic force. It became so tempting to just give in. I was struggling, my chest hurt, I couldn't breathe properly, my arms and legs were flailing and I wasn't going anywhere. I couldn't even feel my body anymore. It felt like I should just stop paddling and allow myself to succumb to the deep dark water. I had to resist that urge. The struggle became so great, that I had to fight against it. There was a temptation to stop as if it was a natural thing to do.

I kept pressing on to my target, there was a small rocky beach, barely visible from the layer of snow that covered the ground, it was only about 40 metres away at this point; the length of 2 small swimming pools.

Underwater currents shuffled below me, tiny hands emerging from the glacial depths, gripping onto my legs and pulling me down into the murky abyss. I tried not to imagine the vast emptiness from below. How peaceful and tranquil it would be to just give in and float down there.

Desperately trying to focus and keep my head above water, I continued paddling with everything I could muster.

Land began to approach; I considered the fact that there may be steep shelves. I decided it would be best to just swim and crash on the beach rather than trying to put my feet down, in case there was no ground below as I would not have the strength to pull myself up.

I hit the beach and kept paddling until my body was lying flat on land. I grasped onto the rocks and could have kissed the dirt below me. Knowing I still needed to re-warm and that my clothes were on the other side of the lake I quickly tried to stand to my feet.

Pressing off with my hands against a rock, I stood tall, stepped forward and stumbled as my legs struggled to support my weight. I fell forward to the ground and cut my feet and hands on a jagged rock. I felt so weak. I pushed myself back up and walked, crouching forward so my arms could support for a few steps until I regained enough strength to walk normally.

My feet crunched on the firm snow and I walked back. I began to shivered and as soon as I got back to my clothes, I put them back on as quick as I could, it was very difficult with the shivering, but I knew that it was vitally important for me to do so. After I wrapped my layers on, I lay on my side and threw up.

Lessons

Don't swim in freezing cold lakes
This was not my brightest idea. I put myself at risk, but also had I gone unconscious, drowned or died I would also have put others at risk. This was stupid and I do not recommend it.

Hopefully this story highlights that in the pursuit of extreme challenge and adventure, it is possible to miscalculate and there could be severe consequences. In this situation as well, the brain can become a bit delusional and I was able to resist the temptation to quit and forego any form of panic. I was also very fortunate that I was able to continue paddling towards the end begin the re-warming process or I could have been in trouble!

22,000 Jumping Jacks
and Injury Strikes

22,000 Jumping Jacks and Injury Strikes

This challenge was to celebrate 22,000 subscribers on YouTube. I'd just start doing jumping jacks until I reached 22,000 – sounds simple enough? This was quite a tough one!

This was undertaken during the third Covid lockdown in the UK. What didn't really help matters was that my Achilles tendons had received an absolute battering as I had been doing countless High Intensity Interval Training sessions online for gym clients and had been taking part in a lot of challenges that involved burpees and running up hills.

It was a very cold day and my tendons were feeling pretty sore before I even started. But I would perform the jumps and mark them off on the board, quite similar to how I did the 1000 pull ups challenge a few years earlier.

It was performed on a live stream and was going quite well. I received a lot of support from people viewing the live stream and from my girlfriend Nez who kept me topped up with coffee.

About three quarters of the way through however, my

tendons were in severe pain. I'd done quite a bit of damage to them, and could barely move my feet. I was determined to finish and the last 1,000 were so painful. I didn't want to let down the people who were watching. My technique changed so that I was bouncing more on my heel then the balls of my feet, to try and lessen the impact on the tendon.

Eventually I hit the 22,000 mark and I was so relieved to finish.

Nez cooked me a warm meal, but it was so cold that I began to rapidly lose body heat. Hypothermia was setting in and I could barely move. I ate food and went to bed, waking up the next morning unable to walk or even move my feet.

This was a make or break moment for me. When the realisation hit me that I had severely damaged both my Achilles tendons for a brief moment all the things I enjoy about life flashed in front of my eyes. Hiking, walking, challenges, training, running and jumping – the movements that we are so gifted with. I thought about the moment that I completed the Car Pull Marathon and the Piano Carry.

For about one second, I felt total despair – I was never going to be able to do these things again.

Then, I flipped the switch. **<u>I will</u>** do those things again.

With that thought in mind, I pulled my phone out, went online and bought myself a pair of £200 hiking boots (I got them a lot cheaper than this though, thanks to veteran's discount!).

My goal would be to build myself back up and then these new boots would be ready and waiting for me to break in as soon as I was strong enough. It gave me a goal and a purpose.

I would have to begin the slow process of rehabilitating my Achilles tendons. I saw this as an opportunity to work towards something. I put together a plan and followed it. Allowing my tendons to rest and heal. Then I began trying to get the range of motion back, before strengthening exercises could begin. As soon as I could walk properly, I'd go for a short walk on a flat surface of around 1,000 steps. Then over time I would gradually increase this distance.

Once I was happy with my progress, I would keep increasing the distance walked but introduce slight inclines and uneven terrain and more strength exercises.

I am pleased to say that my tendons made a swift recovery, however moving forwards I am being much more careful with what I do with them. Any workouts that I deem strenuous on the tendon will always have at least 72 hours rest before I do anything similar.

This served as another lesson to me – that I must focus on the challenges that are important to me. While the 22,000 Jumping Jacks was my challenge, and an important one to me. I had knackered my body out by doing a lot of random challenges that were not taking me in the direction I wanted to go.

Royal Marines Press Up Test

It was a summer day sometime in 2016. I was about to do something that would change the course of my life, set a global trend and inspire thousands of people to work towards a goal.

The **22 Press Ups for #22Kill** challenge was taking social media by storm. It seemed that virtually everyone was doing 22 press ups a day and then tagging their mates to do the same. Within my circle of friends, the individual challenges were becoming more and more outrageous with each passing day as we each tried to outdo each other with better press ups, insane locations and ridiculous variations of press ups.

To celebrate the end of this challenge, I stepped outside to attempt the Royal Marines Press Up test (as performed in recruit training and the Potential Royal Marines Course). It had been eleven years since I had last attempted this test and I wanted to see if I could still complete it.

After bashing out the 60 press ups to the infamous beep, I was pretty pumped, chuffed and in two minds as to whether I should actually post the video or not. I very nearly did not.

I went ahead and uploaded the video and within a few weeks it began to go viral, with people from all over the world attempting it, and also making videos of themselves trying it. This also sent a lot of people my way who were interested in joining the Royal Marines asking for tips on how to improve their fitness and specifically their press ups.

Even to this day I find it quite surreal that millions of people have watched a video of me doing a set of press ups!

The Truck Pull

The Truck Pull

In June 2021, I decided that it was time for me to start gearing up towards a new challenge. I had seen a post online about a charity train pulling event. Having contacted the organiser about taking part and not receiving any response, I took matters into my own hands and decided to create my own event.

Reminiscing about 2019's Car Pull Marathon, I had a few ideas in mind. I wanted to pull something bigger, heavier and harder.

My mind conjured up the idea of pulling a truck over the furthest known distance. This would turn out to be an event that would stress me from all different angles and quite nearly kill me.

I started to tailor my training specifically for pulling objects. I ordered some new footwear for me to test. Grip was going to be vitally important. Concurrently, I was searching for a location to attempt this, a truck for me to pull and a HGV driver. Three months would be sufficient for all this, or so I thought.

My initial plan was to get a truck with a weight of 7.5 tonnes. This would class it as a HGV and then I'd try and pull it for a set distance.

What I hadn't thought was that there would be a shortage of HGV drivers in the UK at this time (apparently due to Covid and Brexit the UK just didn't have enough drivers; deliveries were delayed and petrol pumps were empty).

I made enquiries with countless companies that I could think of, sent email after email; phone call after phone call. No joy finding a location, a truck or a driver.

It was at this point that I had absolutely no idea, what size / weight of vehicle I would get my hands on, or the type of track I could use.

This made my training very difficult as all I knew was that I would be pulling something, somewhere. What piled the pressure on was that I had set up a JustGiving fundraising page; donations were coming in, yet I didn't even know if I was going to be able to do the event!

I had told everyone it was going to be in August at some point – I needed there to be as little chance of rain as possible.

Training consisted of pulling sleds and lots of strength work on the legs and pulling with the upper body in the gym and on the sled. I made my own sled out of a tyre that I would pull along the streets, trails and up hills. I would put lots of weight on top of the tyre and find surfaces with lots of grip to increase friction and make it harder for me to pull.

I thoroughly enjoyed this training. It was tough. I'd use the Bergen from the 100kg / 100km challenge, load it up with weight plates, carry the tyre in my hand for a couple of miles until I reached a suitable training area; and then I'd pull the make shift sled for an hour or so, before walking back. This was done during the height of the Summer, and as usual with my event specific training, random members of the public stopped to kindly ask if I was OK, or in need of help.

As August progressed, I maintained my training on top of my busy working schedule. The date for the event was rapidly approaching and I still did not have any of the three things I needed. Up until four days before the event, I was still ringing around haulage companies asking if they had any spare trucks.

I needed an image of me pulling a truck to help with the fundraising efforts. Renault Trucks in Cardiff kindly allowed me to come up for a photo shoot of me attached to the front of their truck. I still could not get my hands on a truck up North where the event was likely to be held after some promising conversations with my old friend Jase.

My friend came through. He had contacts with Elvington Airfield and access to what he believed was a 10-tonne truck. This was all confirmed a couple of days before the event.

Once it was confirmed, I was able to relax slightly.

The event itself, was scheduled to be in the middle of a mini holiday. Not the brightest idea. We were set to visit friends and also the Peak District for a bit of adventure and sightseeing. We would stop off at Elvington in the middle of this, complete the event and then continue with the holiday. It would be a jam packed four days with lots of driving.

We packed the car with holiday items and my challenge kit. My Bergen was stowed away neatly in the boot filled to the brim with water, snacks, gloves, spare shoes, ropes, shackles, satsumas, banana etc. Everything I needed.

We began the long drive up leaving significantly later than planned. We arrived at our hotel the night before very tired, at around midnight. The bed was not very comfortable and had a terrible night's sleep.

August 25th 2021
Near York
England

After fuelling up with a massive full English breakfast, we checked out of the hotel and the rain started pouring down. I loaded up the car and was trying my hardest to keep my cool. We were running behind schedule and it was raining.

As we started driving towards Elvington Airfield, the rain stopped and the Sun came out. The quiet lanes became an absolute pleasure to drive down and I followed the sat nav until we reached the gates.

It was here that I met Jase and we headed towards the truck. It was a large sweeper. Upon inspecting the vehicle, it became apparent that it was significantly heavier than we had realised as inside the driver's door there was a small plate that said Gross Vehicle Mass: 18 tonnes.

The sweeper had a large tank which did contain water, although it was apparently not fully laden. This meant that the actual weight of the truck was not quite 18 tonnes but it was probably not very far off.

We drove to the start point and I began to warm up and put on my trusty white compression tights and some pink trainers that I thought would be funny to wear.

Elvington is an incredible place. It was perfect for this challenge. At 1.92 Miles, it is one of the longest runways in the UK. As a disused runway, in the middle of nowhere it is just a long straight road surrounded by pure desolation. I loved it.

It is also nearly completely flat. There are slight gradient changes over the near 2-mile length, I imagine this has something to do with the curvature of the Earth, although I am not an expert on the matter.

Standing from one end looking straight down the runway, it is certainly possible to see the gradient change. It raised up slightly, until around the middle, before levelling off and possibly even going down slightly. This gradient change was not drastic, possibly 1% or even less. If the track hadn't been so long and view unobstructed, it would not have been noticeable. That is, until you strap yourself to a heavy goods vehicle and try and pull it.

The plan was to attempt to pull the truck from East to West as I was informed that the wind was likely going to be blowing East to West and would offer less resistance for me. Just as we were starting off, a quick wind check showed that it was going from West to East and blowing against me and the truck. I am not sure how much difference this would have made, so cracked on anyway.

The truck had been parked right at the end of the track and I could that the road here was dipped down slightly as the I could the rear wheels were slightly lower down than the front wheels. This would require a lot of effort to move from this position.

We attached the harness to the front of the truck. Attached an 80ft rope to the rear of my car and drove it in front so the rope was outstretched and lying on the floor in front of. The hand break of the car was firmly applied. I secured myself within the harness, leant into it, dug the tips of my feet into the floor, reached my hands onto the rope so my body was nearly parallel to the floor began pushing with my legs and pulling with my arms at the same time. And nothing happened. The rope began to stretch as I pulled it and my feet slipped and I fell to the floor.

The truck hadn't budged.

I tried again and had the same result.

I just couldn't get enough traction or power to get the truck moving and pull it out of the dip.

The driver of the truck spoke to me and explained the situation, he said he would give a little gas to help break the inertia to get out of this little dip and then leave the rest to me.

This worked, and I have to admit that I felt a bit let down by myself that I had to have some assistance in starting the vehicle at the beginning, but I didn't have time to think. I moved, pushed with my legs as hard as I could, short fast, powerful movements, hand over hand on the rope and trying to let it fall between my legs so that I wouldn't trip over it.

My legs were screaming as I pushed and pushed, like I was sprinting with the shortest stride in the world. Pushing off the floor trying to find grip on any jagged bit of tarmac to help push off. Gaining momentum was the challenging bit, and so even though my legs were on fire, my glutes and quadriceps in particular were screaming – I had to push through the pain until I reached the car and the truck almost immediately ground to a halt behind me.

I reached the car and practically collapsed into the boot. I could barely breathe and my heart was beating out of my chest.

We drove the car forward and repeated the process.

Luckily, the tarmac on Elvington changes a little further up the track. It's more similar to that of a motorway which allows for up to 15x more grip that the bit at the start. This really helped me with my starts, there was less slipping, making the starts a lot more manageable.

Around the 1km point I completed a pull and was keeled over in the boot of my car wheezing. I detached myself from the harness and sat on the floor with my back up against the side of the car and my knees bent. I went cold and start sweating profusely and felt sick. I thought I was about to have a heart attack.

I put myself into this position to reduce strain on my heart and put me in a closer position to the floor should I suddenly collapse. The feeling subsided slightly, but I still felt a little nauseous. After a few minutes I stood up. I was going to be sick now. I walked over to the side of the runway and threw my guts up.

After a brief rest, it was time to crack on with the challenge. Luckily it was at around this point that we had reached the peak of the track, the very slight incline. That, coupled with the change of tarmac made the rest of the pull significantly easier than the first 1km.

As I was not holding down food well, I maintained my energy up with satsumas, water, caffeine, electrolytes, pureed nuts and a huge amount of beta alanine and citrulline. These are amino acids that are often found in pre-workouts.

After 5 hours of pulling in this leap frog manner, the end of the track was in site. My quads and glutes were pumped up to ridiculous levels and it felt like my compression tights were going to burst.

Eventually we reached the end of the track and as I grinded to a halt, the truck stopped abruptly behind me and my quadriceps painfully cramped up. I could not bend my legs for a few minutes and so just stood there while photos were taken, and eventually I was able to bend my legs, stretch them out, remove the harness and hobble off.

After completing this challenge, we had a quick bite to eat, some coffee and then drove us to Macclesfield where we had a lovely hotel with a pool booked. I was hoping to use this for a relax and possible have a massage. During the night my breathing was very laboured and the next day I felt so weak. We were supposed to go exploring the Peak District, but I could barely walk to the end of the street without lying down.

It would take me over 3 weeks before I began to feel normal again. For weeks I could barely stand for long periods of time.

Having checked my heart rate monitor it became apparent that my heart rate had exceeded my theoretical maximum of 186bpm and had spent a significant amount of time in the 200-210 range.

To put things into perspective, during a test I had done on myself I performed all-out hill sprints continuously for around 45 minutes and the highest I could get my heart rate to go was 178bpm. It would seem that this challenge had been incredibly stressful on my heart rather than my muscles and took me a long time to recover.

It would be interesting to have my heart studied one day to see if any long-term damage was done!

Lessons

Don't try to arrange a challenge in the middle of a holiday! It was very stressful trying to arrange this in the middle of a HGV driver crisis and I should have focussed my energy on preparing for and recovering after this challenge.

Fun Facts!

- It took just under 6 hours to complete this challenge;

- At one point, the car hand break was not fully engaged and I was pulling the truck behind me and the car towards me with the rope!

- A total of £580 was raised for the Royal Brompton & Harefield Hospitals Charity.

What Next?

I get asked this all the time. Literally all the time. What am I going to be doing next? I always have some ideas up my sleeve, but at the moment I am just enjoying my training and catching up on work. (This a total lie, I have a few things in mind!!)

You have reached the final pages of the book and I would like to thank you so much for reading and I really hope you enjoyed it, and that it inspires you to challenge yourself to achieve your goals.

As I have said a few times during this book – I am not special, I don't have loads of money. In fact, I have spent most of my life absolutely broke and with my head in my hands trying to figure out how to pay for things.

But what I have been able to do, is get out there and turn my ideas, dreams, goals and aspirations into a reality. While many see their success in terms of careers or finance, for me that is not the case.

If I can aspire to achieve the things that I set out to do, and if my actions can raise money for charity, help people, inspire others to accomplish their goals or raise money for their own chosen charity, that ripple effect is of more value to me than any money in the world.

I'll leave you with these final words. Whatever it is you want to do with your life, get out there and get it done.

Author Profile

Max Glover is a fitness enthusiast who now enjoys writing about his extreme challenges. The former Royal Marine has led a varied and unique life previously working as a maritime security operative and close protection officer and is now a proud ambassador of the mental resilience and running brand Rokman.

With stories to tell and training programmes to write - Max has pushed himself to the limits through a variety of disciplines - running, bodybuilding and calisthenics. Most recently raising thousands of pounds for charity by towing an 18-tonne truck for 2 miles (Furthest known distance), carrying a piano up a mountain, carrying 100kg for 100km (furthest known distance) and towing a 1.7 tonne car for 26.2 miles (smashing the world record at the time).

Max spends his down time relaxing with his family and cats and is most happy these days rucking with a heavy Bergen (military rucksack) enjoying the great outdoors... and is looking forward to sharing his next adventure with you!

<u>More books from Max Glover:</u>

Commando Runner

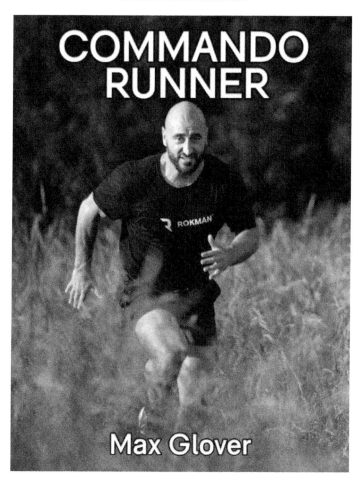

If you want to be the best, then start training like them. Use military training methods to improve your running and specifically your 1.5 mile run time.

Become The Elite

It's no secret - Royal Marines are renowned for their superior levels of physical fitness. This training programme uses methods employed by Commandos to achieve and maintain their elite performance. This guide will help If you are looking to join any branch of the military, run a 10k, obstacle course race, half marathon, if you are currently serving and looking to gain an edge over your peers or just improve your physical fitness.

- Comprehensive day by day training programme to follow - Be ready for anything

- How to optimise performance - Unlock the power of your mind

- Nutrition information - get the best out of your food

- Exercise and stretching guide - Activate and strengthen your muscles

- Fitness Testing - watch your times improve

Written by a former Royal Marine and extreme challenge athlete Max Glover

  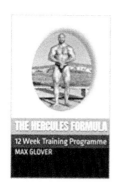

Commando90 – a 90 day no BS guide to obtain a Commando level of fitness. This is raw and basic, suitable for those who just want to follow a guide without any unnecessary distractions. Intense circuit training sessions for different abilities. Can be completed with bodyweight only and no fancy gym equipment.

Challenge What You Think, Believe What is Possible – Max Glover lets you into his mind while he completes unique challenges, such as carrying a piano up a mountain, towing a car for a marathon and much more. He explains how he trained for each challenge and also valuable lessons and insights from his time in the Royal Marines. (Kindle Edition)

The Hercules Formula – This is a 12 week bodybuilding programme with the sole purpose of getting bigger and stronger using weights.

Image credits: Rokman www.rokman.co.uk
@teamrokman

Instagram: @muscle.world.fitness

Printed in Great Britain
by Amazon

83502510R00195